THE ULTIMATE
ST. LOUIS CARDINALS
BASEBALL CHALLENGE

THE ULTIMATE ST. LOUIS CARDINALS BASEBALL CHALLENGE

David Nemec

and

Scott Flatow

TAYLOR TRADE PUBLISHING

Lanham • New York • Boulder • Toronto • Plymouth, UK

Published by Taylor Trade Publishing
An imprint of The Rowman & Littlefield Publishing Group, Inc.
4501 Forbes Boulevard, Suite 200, Lanham, Maryland 20706
www.rlpgtrade.com

Distributed by NATIONAL BOOK NETWORK

Library of Congress Cataloging-in-Publication Data

Nemec, David.
    The ultimate St. Louis Cardinals baseball challenge / David Nemec
and Scott Flatow.
        p. cm.
    ISBN-13: 978-1-58979-349-1 (pbk. : alk. paper)
    ISBN-10: 1-58979-349-8 (pbk. : alk. paper)
    1. St. Louis Cardinals (Baseball team)—Miscellanea. I. Flatow, Scott,
1966– II. Title.

GV875.S3N46 2008
796.357'640977866—dc22   2007041429

Manufactured in the United States of America.

CONTENTS

GAME 4

GAME 5

GAME 6

GAME 7

ACKNOWLEDGMENTS

The authors would like to thank Dave Zeman, Dick Thompson, and Al Blumkin for their help in fact-checking this book and offer special thanks and appreciation to Cliff Blau for providing a fourth pair of fact-checking eyes that would do even an eagle proud.

FOREWORD

I am honored to write the foreword for this groundbreaking series of baseball quiz books by Scott Flatow and David Nemec. I first encountered Scott at the Society for American Baseball Research (SABR) New York City regional meeting in 1985. He wrote an especially challenging and compelling baseball quiz for the event, which I consider myself very fortunate to have won. We became close friends soon after that meeting. Scott quickly went on to bigger and better things as both a baseball trivia player and an author. In recent years he has won three SABR National Trivia championships (two team and one individual). Scott's 1995 team set the current SABR team record for the widest margin of victory, and he later posted the highest individual score to date when he won the individual competition in 2001. During that span he also co-authored *The Macmillan Baseball Quiz Book* and penned *The McFarland Baseball Quiz Book*. In addition, he has written numerous quizzes for independent publications.

In 1991, Scott received a call from Steve Nadel, the New York City SABR chapter chairman and host of that year's National convention in New York City, informing him that David Nemec was planning to attend a SABR convention for the first time. Scott immediately contacted me and we both became very excited because David is recognized to be the father of baseball trivia. He had written two books in the late 1970s, *The Absolutely Most Challenging Baseball Quiz Book, Ever* and *The Even More Challenging Baseball Quiz Book*, that are now regarded as the pioneering works in the field. Scott and I first met David in June of 1991 at the SABR New York City National convention for which Scott orchestrated the trivia competition. As a first-time player, David helped his team to narrowly defeat my team in the finals, and an instant bond developed between us.

In addition to *The Absolutely Most Challenging Baseball Quiz Book, Ever* and *The Even More Challenging Baseball Quiz Book*, David is the author of more than 25 baseball books including two quiz books in the 1990s, the indispensable *The Great Encyclopedia of Nineteenth Century Major League Baseball* and *The Beer and Whisky League*, which ranks as the seminal work on the American Association in the years that it was a major league. David is also the co-holder with me of a record seven SABR National Trivia Championships. He has won six team competitions as well as the first individual championship in 1995.

The matchless qualities in David Nemec's and Scott Flatow's new series of team quiz books are their wry wit, their amazing scope, and, above all, the fact that they not only test a reader's recall, they also force him or her to think out of the box and in so doing to expand his or her knowledge of our national game. You will never find such tired posers as "Who pitched the only perfect game in the World Series?" or "What year did the Dodgers move to Los Angeles?" Instead you will be constantly challenged to test the depth and breadth of your baseball knowledge from the first major league baseball game in 1871 to the present day. Furthermore, in this unique series of quiz books you are certain to learn a wealth of new information about players ranging from the well known like Babe Ruth and Hank Aaron to such inimitably ephemeral performers as Eddie Gaedel and Shooty Babbit.

In short, Nemec and Flatow inform as well as entertain. Most other quiz books are content to lob questions at you without helping to guide you toward the answer. You either know who hit such and such, or you don't. Your only recourse if you don't is to consult the answer section, shrug, and move on. Nemec and Flatow take a very different approach. First they toss a tantalizing and oftentimes completely original teaser to set your synapses firing. Then they crank your brain up to full boil with descriptive clues that are deftly designed to steer the savvy mind toward the answer. And fair warning: the answer is all too often a name that

will make you whack your forehead and go, "Wow, how did I ever miss that?" Have fun with these books. I never had so much fun in all my long years as a trivia aficionado.

Alan Blumkin is the only man to win two consecutive individual SABR National trivia championships. In addition, he has made numerous historical presentations at both local and National SABR conventions. He lives in Brooklyn, New York, and is currently resting on his laurels while serving as the chief administrator and question contributor for the annual SABR National championships.

INTRODUCTION

How dare we call this the ultimate St. Louis Cardinals baseball challenge?

First and foremost, it's been designed to give you, our dear reader, the four things you most want in a baseball quiz book: (1) pleasure; (2) a worthy challenge; (3) an opportunity to learn something new about the game you love and the team that, chances are, many of you find at once endearing and eternally frustrating; (4) the assurance that you're in the company of quiz masters who know their stuff. In short, you not only want to match wits, you also like to come away from a book like this with the feeling that you've been enlightened in the bargain. You will be, you have our guarantee, by the time you finish here.

What we've assembled is a seven-game World Series of entertainment, innings one through nine, starting off with rookies and ending with famous Fall Classic events and heroes. There's a logic to our structure, of course, as there is to all the categories we've chosen. In fact, we'll alert you right off the bat, as it were, that to score well against our curves, drops, and heat you need to be moderately savvy in every on-the-field phase of the Cardinals' rich history: from the infant days of the franchise, when the team was in the rebel American Association and known as the Browns, to the final pitch delivered last season.

That isn't to say, though, that you've got to have a raft of stats and a host of obscure players at your fingertips. Actually, top marks are there for the taking by anyone who has a reasonable amount of knowledge of the game in general coupled with a good eye for using our clues to zero in on the right answer to even our seemingly all but impossible questions. And speaking of stats, our authority for those we use is the current edition of *The*

ESPN Baseball Encyclopedia except in the very rare instances where that reference work conflicts with the authors' own research findings. Similarly, our authorities for issues like what constitutes rookie status, batting title eligibility, and other such matters are the current major league rules except in cases where we've alerted you that a different criterion is being used.

Before ushering you behind the curtain and showing you how our minds work, first let us show you an example of the type of question we abhor: What Kansas City Royals batter hit into the first triple play in Seattle Mariners history and what Mariner recorded the last out in the play? Unless you happened to see that particular play (which is highly unlikely) or else have a PhD in triple plays (also unlikely), all you can do is throw up your hands and take a couple of wild guesses as to who the two players are. And where's the fun in that? However, if the question had also provided the clues that the Royals batter now resides in the Hall of Fame and the Mariner who recorded the last out in the triple play spent most of his career as a backup catcher in the mid-1970s with the Astros, then all the burners would be fired and the question would be a fair one to ask, albeit still not one to our taste.

In short, that's our approach. A good question doesn't just toss up a mildly interesting but essentially arcane feat. It gives you a reasonable opportunity to nail the player or players who were involved in it by providing enough information about them to allow you to make at least an educated guess. Hall of Famer? Could be Harmon Killebrew who finished his career in KC. But wait! Was Killebrew still around when the Mariners came into existence? No. Then who was? We won't spoil the fun by giving away the answer any more than we'll spill on the 'stros backup catcher, but now you get the idea how we work.

Here we are cobbling away in our workshop on three different levels of questions that are more to our taste:

SIMPLE: Who is the only Cardinal to win more than one batting title with a 400+ batting average? Single.

INTERMEDIATE: In the 1946 World Series whose hit brought home Enos Slaughter with the winning run in the seventh and deciding game? True Cards fans will cakewalk to a double here.

EXPERT: The last-place 1898 St. Louis NL entry experienced almost a complete roster turnover when syndicate ownership brought every major contributor on the 1898 Cleveland Spiders westward to the Mound City the following year. Only two regulars on the 1898 St. Louis club played enough for the 1899 outfit to qualify for either the ML batting title or ERA crown that year by dint of their St. Louis stats alone. Both began that season with the awful emaciated 1899 version of the Spiders before the dual ownership shifted their talents to St. Louis. One was a position player, the other a pitcher. You need both to tag a three-run homer.

Question 1 is so easy that it merits no clues and rates only a single.

In question 2 you're given an inkling that it just might contain a clue if it's read carefully. Good for you if you've already spotted that our clues sometimes come in the form of wordplay or puns.

The reward in question 3 is among the highest offered in our book. In addition, you get a sampling of the standard abbreviations we use. Here they're NL, short for National League, ML, short for major league, and ERA, short for earned run average. Elsewhere you'll encounter other standard abbreviations such as AL for American League, PCL for Pacific Coast League, AB for at bats, BA for batting average, OBP for on base percentage, SA for slugging average, PA for plate appearances, and OPS for on base percentage plus slugging average.

We won't spoil your fun by giving away the answers to our sample questions. Consider them a bonus. And, incidentally, there are a number of other bonuses in our book, not the least of which is our invitation to compile your own BA, SA, and RBI total as you go along. There are roughly 900 plate appearances in *The*

Ultimate St. Louis Cardinals Baseball Challenge. Don't expect to hit above .300, though, unless you really know your Redbirds. But by the same token, you have our assurance that not even diehard Mound City fans are likely to outhit readers who have a firm knowledge of all of major league history. This, after all, is the ultimate Cardinals test for the ultimate well-rounded fan.

Now enjoy.

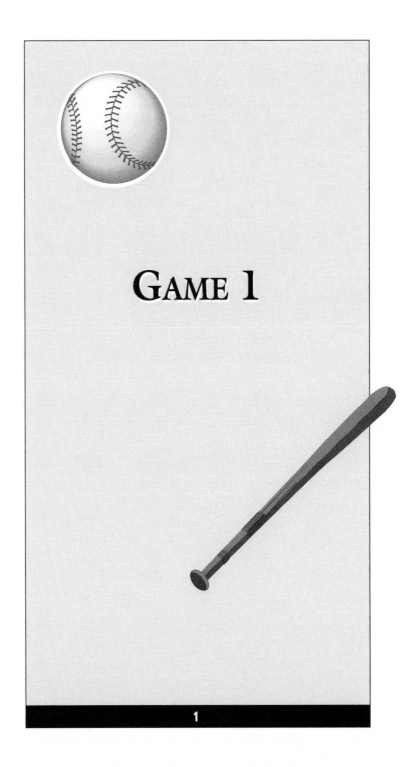

GAME 1

INNING 1
RED-HOT ROOKIES

1 His rookie year saw him clock in at 9–13 with the Cards in 201 innings. The remaining 13 years of his career produced 230 wins and only 117 losses. Unhappily, nary a one of those 230 victories came in Cards flannels. Name this Birds hurler who fled the coop after his frosh season and landed in the Hall of Fame with a .648 career winning percentage and bank a deuce, plus a ribby for his lone year as a Bird.

2 What Cards rookie led all ML frosh in appearances with 67 but really opened eyes that year by becoming the first documented hurler to belt a homer as a pinch hitter on the first pitch he ever saw in the majors? A year later he was gone for good. RBI single, plus an extra ribby for the year he became an all too fleeting memory.

3 These two St. Louis yearling tossers were a combined 22–8. The following year they bagged 73 wins between them. Needless to say, they were St. Louis's Big Two that year, and two is all you historians get if you recognize both from our scant clues, plus a RBI for their frosh season.

4 The only Cardinal to slug .600+ as a rookie (minimum 502 PA) is worth just a single on the streets of St. Louis—or anywhere else, for that matter.

5 What 20-year-old frosh hit .315 for the Cards in 140 games and topped his rookie season 20 years later at age 40 by hitting .330? Both figures wound up being *below* his career BA. More than enough clues for true Birds fans to smack a single up the middle, plus a RBI for the frosh year we've cited here.

6 The 1928 NL flag winner was a veteran team with one notable exception. What rookie outfielder smacked .341 in 68 games? A St. Louis native, he failed to appear in the World Series with the Cards that year but returned to the team in 1931 in time to see fall action against the Philadelphia A's. The owner of a .285 career BA in eight seasons, he rates a three-run homer.

7 Standing 6'5", this 24-year-old Cards righty bagged a NL rookie-leading 13 wins while also topping senior-loop frosh in winning percentage, starts, innings, and strikeouts. This Indiana-born lad never again qualified for an ERA title after shoulder surgery ruined him, and he closed his career with the 2003 Rangers. RBI single, plus an extra RBI for his first full season.

8 Here's another 6'5" Cards chucker who paced NL freshmen in victories, winning percentage, starts, innings, strikeouts, and ERA. Although he underwent Tommy John surgery, this righty thrived upon returning and even started a Series game in a losing effort with the Birds before the lure of free-agent greenbacks pulled him elsewhere. Single, plus a RBI for his rookie season.

9 Who was the most recent hurler to win 20 games as a Cards rookie? Even with the info that he failed to win top rookie honors in the NL that year, though he was eligible, you still can earn a two-bagger, plus a RBI for his rookie year.

10 Do you remember the St. Louis native who went 10–6 with a nifty 2.53 ERA and a team-leading 10 complete games as a frosh for Ken Boyer's boys, only to bag just four more wins before vanishing at age 24? Double.

11 Name the longtime minor leaguer who was approaching his 30th birthday when the Cards found themselves short an outfielder in the spring of 1930. Platooning held him to just 391 at bats his rookie season, rendering him a nonqualifier for the batting crown by today's rules and thereby depriving his .373 mark of the record for the highest BA ever by a NL frosh. All you should need to bang a double.

12 Rookies took the hill at the beginning of just about every game for the Cards in 1902. Which frosh led the club with 37 starts, 39 appearances, and 21 losses? A product of the Pennsylvania State League, he first surfaced with John McGraw's Baltimore Orioles in 1901 and was last seen in the second game of the 1903 season when Cards skipper Patsy Donovan excused him after the fifth inning when he trailed Chicago 6–0, thanks to being victimized for five unearned runs. Under the quixotic scoring rules of the time, he was charged with the 7–6 loss even though the Cards later tied the game, only to lose it in the 10th inning. Three-run homer.

13 When he joined the Cards in 1920, he was the Birds' last rookie of consequence for nearly two decades who was not a product of the club's vast farm system. And he was indeed of consequence, as he parlayed his 13 frosh wins into a 19-year career that led to the pinnacle in Cooperstown. RBI single.

14 In 1936 the Cards unveiled two rooks who truly book-ended the Birds' season. One debuted on Opening Day and became the first player to knock a pinch homer in his initial ML at bat, doing it on the first pitch to boot. It was his lone big league tater, and he quickly faded into baseball oblivion. The other got his first taste of big league action on closing day that year after Johnny Mize's late-game ejection summoned him off the bench to anchor first base for the Cards and fan in his only career at bat. However, unlike the other rook, this one-at-bat sub now resides in Cooperstown. Now, here's the real book-ender! Both yearlings faced the *same* pitcher in their initial ML at bats, and that twirler would lead the Cards in wins the following year, with 18, after arriving in the Mound City via a trade. Triple for all three performers, double for two, zilch for anything less.

AB: 14
Hits: 14
Total Bases: 27
RBI: 16

INNING 2
WHAT WAS THEIR REAL HANDLE?

How many of the real first names of these Cards do you know?

1 Bernard Gilkey. Tough double.

2 Wattie Holm. Two-run homer.

3 Red Schoendienst. Should be a routine single.

4 Tino Martinez. Single.

5 Rip Repulski. RBI double.

6 Vinegar Bend Mizell. Just a single for this familiar chestnut.

7 Nippy Jones. Two-run single.

8 Albert Pujols. Single.

9 Pepper Martin. Double.

10 Dal Maxvill. RBI double.

11 Rocky Nelson. RBI double.

12 Whitey Kurowski. Double.

13 Slim Sallee. Solo homer.

14 Solly Hemus. Two-run double.

15 J. D. Drew. Two-run single.

AB: 15
Hits: 15
Total Bases: 28
RBI: 12

THE ULTIMATE ST. LOUIS CARDINALS BASEBALL CHALLENGE

INNING 3
MASTER MOUNDSMEN

1 A charitable single bounces your way in the form of the only Card to date who worked 200+ innings for six straight seasons. Add two RBI if you know the six-year span.

2 The first hurler to lead either the NL or the AL in ERA with a figure above 3.00 was a redheaded St. Louis southpaw who was born, bred, and died in the Mound City. Name him for a double, plus a RBI for the year he paced the NL in ERA.

3 Who was the last twirler to win 20 games on a Cards club that featured Lou Brock? Our tosser rebounded after an 8–10 showing with the Redbirds to go 20–7 in Brock's coda, only to crash at 11–17 the next year. Single for this seesaw starter, plus a RBI for the year he bagged 20.

4 The first Cards hurler to notch two NL ERA crowns was also one of the first players to have his name appear on a new ball-glove model. Worth a single, and a RBI for each of the two years he won the crown.

5 During a season in which he turned 37, this righty posted a career-best 18 wins to lead the Cards in victories and earn his first All-Star berth. A year later he was bombed for seven runs, all earned in just 2⅓ frames during his lone Redbirds Series start before exiting the club via free agency. Single, plus a RBI for his standout St. Loo season.

6 To date, he is the only Cards pitcher to win in double figures for five straight seasons under Tony La Russa's glare. During that span he notched 79 victories and over 100 total before departing the Mound City. Single, plus a RBI for his five-season skein.

7 Nail the lone southpaw to rack up a 20-win season in Cards garb between the beginning of the Spanish-American War and the end of World War II. He won 153 altogether for the Birds after debuting in the year that marked the end of World War I. Double.

8 In his second full season up top, this Card led the NL with a 2.52 ERA yet went a modest 11–9 in 30 starts. After toiling for three other teams, he retired with 123 victories, the most to date by an Arizona-born hurler. RBI single, plus an extra base for the year he paced the senior loop in ERA.

9 When Dizzy Dean won 30 games in 1934, whose post-1892 Cards franchise record did he break for the most victories in a season? Our clue is that the mark of 27 was set in the same year Hugh Duffy hit a record .440. Double, plus a RBI for the year.

10 Which of these pitchers never led or shared the lead on a Cards team in victories? Bryn Smith, Three Finger Brown, Rich DeLucia, John Stuper, Curt Simmons, Jeff Suppan, Dave LaPoint. RBI single.

11 Who was the lone St. Louis NL hurler prior to Dizzy Dean's arrival to log a season in which he fanned three or more batters per walk? Those who know both Cards history and early-day hurlers who possessed great control will score a two-bagger here, plus a RBI for the year he had 3.19 Ks for every free pass he issued.

12 Using the current criteria for determining loop winning percentage leaders, Bob Gibson led the NL in winning percentage just once during his illustrious career. For a single, in what year did he take top honors?

13 Hurlers who both win and lose 20 games in the same season are a rare breed. One such tosser did it not just once but twice with a St. Louis NL club—and in back-to-back seasons at that! He broke in under a manager named Harry Wright and later managed under an owner named Comiskey. Clues are there for a RBI triple.

14 After Gibby, it would be a while before another Cards qualifier topped the NL in winning percentage (again, using the current criteria for determining loop winning percentage leaders). We'll note that this moundsman went 16–5 (.762) and his nifty 2.16 ERA placed him second in the senior loop that campaign. RBI single, plus a bonus ribby for the year.

> **AB:** 14
> **Hits:** 14
> **Total Bases:** 21
> **RBI:** 15

INNING 4
GOLD GLOVE GOLIATHS

1 Mark a RBI single in your scorebook for pegging the only Cards first sacker to bag six straight Gold Glove Awards. He played in All-Star Games during four of those ingot-winning seasons and stroked over 1,000 hits during that six-year span.

2 The first Card to snare a Gold Glove lapped up four in a row at one point. The clue that his brother later won a NL Gold Glove—and at the same position, no less—makes this only a single, plus a RBI for his brother's name and team with whom he won.

3 Who set a new Cards record for outfield putouts in 1926 and two years later broke his own club mark by a margin of over 100 putouts in the process of setting a new ML standard for outfield putouts that has never been surpassed? RBI single.

4 What gardener won Gold Glove honors in each of his first six seasons with the Cards after bagging two such awards in the AL?

Single, plus a RBI for his six-year bullion-run in the Mound City.

5 Never on a pennant winner, he leads all Cards hurlers with 808 career assists and 935 total chances. The knowledge that he was also the first twirler in Cards franchise history to win as many as 140 games for the Birds should get you in for a RBI single.

6 Who held the Cards club mark for the most Gold Gloves won before the arrival of Ozzie Smith? Only a single, but add an extra base for knowing the total our man earned.

7 The first receiver in ML history to catch as many as 100 games in a season wore the uniform of the Cards' American Association ancestor. Name him for triple, plus two RBI for the year he first broke the century mark and added to his dossier by leading his league in fielding average.

8 The first Cards shortstop to win a Gold Glove did it with a Redbirds flag winner and posted a fielding average *more* than 680 percentage points above his slugging average that season. Single, plus a RBI for the year.

9 Currently nine of the Cards' top 10 season fielding averages by a catcher in a minimum of 100 games belong to post-expansion receivers. Nail the lone pre-expansion member on the list whose .996 mark in 1954 remained the club standard until 1967. He had an even .300 to boot that year, his first of two campaigns as the Birds' regular mitt man. RBI Double.

10 Ozzie Smith broke Marty Marion's club record for the most career assists by a shortstop. What Cardinals shortstop's career record did Marion break? Even with the clue that he played on a Birds flag bearer and later managed pennant winners with two other franchises, we'll kick in a double.

11 Which one of these performers to date has never won a Gold Glove with the Cards? Albert Pujols, Edgar Renteria, Mike Shannon, Ken Reitz, Willie McGee, Scott Rolen. Single.

12 Who holds the Cards season record for catching in the highest percentage of games played by the club? He backstopped in

120+ games in four straight seasons for the Birds, with his high of 147 to set the team's pre-expansion receivers record. RBI double, plus an extra base for his record year.

13 He holds the record for the most Gold Gloves won at his position, with the first five coming in Cards garb. Perhaps the finest fielder ever at that spot, he's worth a single.

14 The first man to play as many as 1,000 games in a St. Louis suit at any of the nine positions is in the Hall of Fame even though he compiled a weak .293 career OBP. Name him and the position he defended so expertly for a single.

AB: 14
Hits: 14
Total Bases: 20
RBI: 10

INNING 5
RBI RULERS

1 Who currently holds the Cards franchise record for the most RBI in a season? Single, plus a RBI for the year he set the mark, and an extra base if you know the record figure.

2 We can't award more than a single for naming the Card who currently holds the NL season record for most RBI by a player with fewer than 250 at bats. But we'll add a generous RBI for the year.

3 Name the first Card to drive in as many as 150 runs in a season. Single for him, plus a RBI for his big year.

4 When he drove in his 721st run with the Cards, he surpassed Frankie Frisch's club career record for most RBI by a switch-hitter.

Sharing that he closed with 929 ribbies in a Birds uniform and still had enough in his lumber to accumulate over 400 more elsewhere rates this a single.

5 In a five-year period, he played on three Cards flag bearers but never led the team in RBI during any of their pennant-winning seasons. However, he did top the Redbirds in ribbies in between their Series appearances in consecutive campaigns with 83 and 78 when they placed seventh and sixth, respectively. This three-time All-Star's good for a RBI single.

6 Between Bobby Wallace's 91 RBI in 1901 and Rogers Hornsby's 94 RBI in 1920, no Cardinal collected as many as 90 ribbies in a season. Who produced 88 RBI in 1914, the club's best figure during the Deadball Era? He played first and short for the most part that year but began his career as a second sacker playing beside the NL's best shortstop at that time. RBI triple for him, plus an extra RBI for his original keystone partner.

7 Who holds the Cards record for the most RBI in a season without leading the NL that year in ribbies? Although he fell 11 shy of the lead, his total was the highest by a Redbird in over 60 years. The following year our man equaled his ribby total and this time topped the senior circuit. Single.

8 The first member of the Cards franchise to log two 100 RBI seasons held the all-time club season RBI record for 34 years with 123. Name him for two bases, plus an extra base for the year of his highwater RBI mark.

9 Who was the most recent player to lead the NL in RBI while performing on a Cards flag bearer? It was his second ribby crown, with the first coming earlier that decade for another NL pennant winner. RBI single.

10 Whose Cards career RBI record of 1,148 did Stan Musial break en route to setting the current club mark of 1,951? Two-bagger.

11 Who was the Cards' lone 100 RBI man during Tony La Russa's first year as Redbirds skipper? This righty stick pushed across 104 that year, and he would lead a NL pennant winner in another city with 115 RBI later that decade. Single, plus a RBI for the year he topped La Russa's crew.

12 Prior to NL expansion in 1962, four Cardinals topped the senior loop in RBI on more than one occasion. Name all four for a double.

13 Among performers who played at least 1,000 games in a Cards uniform, his 231 RBI stands as the lowest total in Birds history. Still, he played in four World Series, three of them as a Card. Double.

14 Prior to 1970, just once in their long history had the Cardinals owned a catcher who tabulated as many as 80 RBI in a season—81 to be exact. He also hit .318 that year, smoked nine home runs, and tied for the club lead in ribbies. Four years later he had his biggest season, clubbing 35 homers with 122 RBI, but it was for another NL team. Milk those clues to get the receiver for two bases, his big year with the Cards for a RBI, and the club with whom he had his career year for a second ribby.

AB: 14
Hits: 14
Total Bases: 23
RBI: 10

INNING 6
PEERLESS PILOTS

1 No NL club has ever won more regular season games, only to be swept in that year's World Series, than a certain Cards club guided by a certain skipper. Single, but you need the manager and the year to reach first.

2 Do you know the lone man to pilot four straight St. Louis pennant winners in any major league? Double, but you also have to know his four-year reign.

3 Who was the only Cards pennant-winning skipper to date that never played in the majors? RBI single.

4 Although the Cards placed last in the NL East in 1990, they did not own the worst record in the senior loop, but it took three skippers to lead them there. Who was the last pilot to steer the Cards into the cellar while they finished with the league's worst record? He did it all by his lonesome, and it was his only year at the Birds helm before giving way to Branch Rickey. Triple.

5 He managed the Cards to 101 victories in his third season as Birds skipper after placing one game under .500 during his freshman year in the Mound City. In his final full managerial season the Redbirds finished 29 games behind a Phillies squad that bagged 101 wins. Who is he for a single?

6 To date, who is the only owner of the Cards franchise to take a crack at running the team himself? He tried it on three different occasions, no less, and logged a dismal 3–14 career record as a pilot. Two-bagger.

7 He currently holds the distinction of being the Cards' most recent skipper to lead them to winning records in each of his first three full seasons at their helm. Single.

8 Name the outfielder that owner Chris Von der Ahe put at the controls of the very first team in Cards franchise history—the 1882 St. Louis Browns—and win a two-run homer. A Philadelphia native and a member of the 1871 Philadelphia Athletics, the first pennant winner in ML history, he liked St. Louis so well that he made it his home until his death in 1905.

9 Who managed the Birds during Lou Brock's final season? RBI single.

10 He was the last man to be able to claim that he guided both the Cards and the Browns during his managerial career. Double.

For an extra base, what was especially significant about his year with the Browns?

11 Who is the only big league pilot that managed Jim Bottomley while he was a member of both the NL Cardinals and the AL St. Louis Browns? A bit of thought will enable the savvy to crown themselves with a RBI two-bagger.

12 He is the only man to date to pitch for the Cards and later manage them to a flag. Double for him, an extra base for the year he won.

13 Who ceded the Cards pilot's job to Rogers Hornsby in 1925 after the season was already under way? The clue that he had a longer tenure with the Redbirds franchise than Hornsby did rates this only a double.

14 Name the only position player on the Cards' first NL flag winner in 1926 to pilot them later to a pennant and capture a RBI double.

> **AB:** 14
> **Hits:** 14
> **Total Bases:** 28
> **RBI:** 6

INNING 7
HOME RUN KINGS

1 To date, only one performer in Cards franchise history has been the club leader in home runs on two Redbirds World Championship teams. There are plenty of names to choose from here, and we're wagering a RBI deuce that you'll choose wrong.

2 Rogers Hornsby hit 30 or more homers in a season twice as a Card. Who were the four other sluggers able to claim even one

30-homer season with the Birds prior to World War II? Triple for all four, single for knowing just three.

3 It would be a while after Stan Musial slammed 35 taters in 1954 before another Card equaled The Man's heady season total. For a RBI single, what slugger at long last matched Musial? Grab an extra base for the year.

4 Who was the first member of the Cards franchise to achieve double-digit totals in the same season in home runs, triples, and doubles? Even just a sliver of knowledge of the franchise's early years should bring you a RBI single, plus another RBI for the year he did it.

5 Set your sights on the first Redbird to blast 20 or more homers in three consecutive seasons. Even our sharing that he played on four Cards Series entrants still rates this a solid RBI double.

6 Who led or shared the Cardinals team lead in homers on five occasions but never went deep more than 26 times in a season as a Bird? His first big league at bat came at age 19 with a Redbirds flag winner, and 14 years later he hammered two round-trippers against the Cards in fall action. RBI single.

7 At the close of the Deadball Era in 1919, who held the record for the most career home runs by a member of the St. Louis NL entry? All we'll add is that his mark of 36 was broken in 1921. Two for him, plus a RBI for the man who eclipsed his club mark.

8 What aging swatter turned 38 the year he broke Stan Musial's club standard for the oldest Redbird to pelt 20+ homers in a season? Few fans realize that he lasted 20 seasons in the bigs and pummeled 360 seat-reachers in over 2,500 games. RBI single for him, plus an extra ribby for his Cards record-setting campaign.

9 Which of these Hall of Famers cranked the most career home runs as a member of the Cards franchise? Charlie Comiskey, Bobby Wallace, Jesse Burkett, Miller Huggins, Leo Durocher, Tommy McCarthy. Bloop double.

10 Who blasted the most homers cumulatively in Cards garb in the decade of the 1990s (1991–2000)? Easy to go wrong here so we'll award a RBI single.

11 The first performer to crash as many as 10 home runs in a season in a St. Louis NL uniform creamed 12 taters in 1894, belying his nickname of "Bones." A shortstop by trade, he finished his long career with the 1902 Washington AL club. Triple.

12 To date, no Card has experienced a 40-homer season without collecting at least 100 RBI. However, a certain Birds slugger pounded out 39 jacks and plated less than 90 mates. Just a single, but add a RBI for the year.

13 Who was the first Mound City NL home run king subsequent to St. Louis's joining the senior loop in 1892? He rates only a single, plus a RBI for the year he was the club's first tater champ.

14 His 11 round-trippers were the fewest to lead a Cards unit in more than 70 years, and that number proved to be prophetic, as he became the first player in ML history to crack at least one dinger with 11 different teams. Single for this suitcase packer, and a RBI for his low-total leadership year.

15 The senior loop record for the most homers by a player in his final ML season belongs to a bammer who finished his career in Cards garb. For a single, who is it?

AB: 15
Hits: 15
Total Bases: 24
RBI: 13

INNING 8
STELLAR STICKWIELDERS

1 Among performers collecting at least 1,000 at bats with the Cardinals, his .378 mark in St. Loo togs reigns supreme. Careful here; it may not be the obvious knee-jerk answer. Infield single.

2 He tied a ML season record (since broken) by slapping 24 pinch hits with the Cards while stroking a composite .311 BA in 183 at bats across 111 games. Although he spent less than two seasons in Redbirds flannels, this 5'7" Venezuelan gardener logged 16 years in the bigs. Two-run single.

3 Catchers who have won batting crowns can be counted on the fingers of one hand. For many years, however, receivers who were bat-title candidates were customarily treated with leniency, especially in seasons when they played as many as 100 games. What Cards backstopper would have forced NL officials to think long and hard before rejecting his candidacy if he had played in just eight more contests when he hit a crackling .399 in 92 games? In his eight-year career he divided his time between wearing a mask and mitt and an outfield glove, finishing with the 1948 Phils. Two-run double, plus an extra base for his near .400 year.

4 Who currently holds the Cards club record for total bases in a season while hitting below .300? No more than a single, once you think about it, but we'll add a RBI for the year.

5 When Ted Simmons rapped .332 in 1975, whose ancient Cards franchise mark for the best season BA by a performer who played the majority of his games that season at catcher (minimum 400 AB) did he break? Pack up the clue that he played 61 games that season behind the plate as opposed to 44 in the outfield and 17 at first base and then head "North to Alaska" where you can surprise everyone with a solo homer, plus two extra ribbies for his big year.

6 The Cards have sported several fine switch-hitters in their long history. Who among them holds the club's switch-stick mark for the most hits in a season? RBI single, plus an extra base for the year.

7 Gents like Bob Caruthers, Dave Foutz, and Jack Stivetts compiled some fine BAs in the Cards' days as a member of the American Association. Yet none of them holds the club record for the highest season BA by a pitcher with a minimum of 100 plate appearances. It belongs to a hurler who collected 22 wins to combine with his heady .381 average for a Redbirds club that featured a first sacker who won the NL batting title that year with a mark 32 points lower than our pitcher's. The hitting hillman will bring a triple, plus an extra base for the bat titlist provided you also know the year he won.

8 Only one hurler with a minimum of 300 at bats as a Cardinal has registered a .250+ career BA since the club joined the National League in 1892. Frequently used as a pinch hitter, he struck a nifty .271 as a moundsman and .255 overall, just eight points less than his younger brother, who caught in the American League in the 1910s and 1920s. Solo homer.

9 Prior to the late 1970s, who was the only man in Cards history to post a .300+ career batting average with a minimum of 1,000 at bats while serving as a shortstop? He's in the Hall of Fame, and if you know the career profiles of Cards Famers, this will be a routine single. Extra base if you can nail his Cards career BA as a shortstop within two points.

10 Who is the only Hall of Fame first sacker to log a .300+ BA with a minimum of 1,000 career at bats as a member of St. Louis NL clubs prior to the end of the Deadball Era in 1919? Your clues are that he was a lefty all the way, and his last career home run came with St. Louis and established a ML mark that stood for the next two decades. RBI single, but only if you also know who broke his ML record.

11 Counting everyone with a minimum of 600 PA in a season, his .306 OBP is the lowest for a first baseman in Cardinal franchise history. He did it with a Redbirds flag winner and, believe it or not, his name isn't Comiskey. Even more incredible is the fact that the previous year in Cards garb he had finished just five percentage points behind the NL OBP leader. Double, plus a RBI for his retrograde season.

12 If the Cards ever were to name their all-time switch-hitters All-Star team, who would be the clear-cut selection at first base? The only clue serious Cards fans will need is that he stood just 5'9". Double.

13 Who holds the Cards season record for the most doubles by a third baseman? His 49 two-baggers left him two shy of a teammate who led the NL in doubles that year. What's more, our hot-corner man, upon his arrival with the Cards, actually displaced that same league leader at third. Single for the record holder, a RBI for naming the teammate who vacated third, plus an extra base for the year.

14 Subsequent to 1892, when St. Louis first joined the NL, just one man bagged as many as 100 RBI in a season in St. Louis NL threads prior to the end of the Deadball Era in 1919. No fly-by-nighter, he was a Mound City mainstay for almost that entire period. Double for him; RBI for his 100-ribby season.

15 Who drilled the most career hits in Cards garb without ever leading the club in that category? Would you believe that he once topped the NL in hits while playing elsewhere and yet did *not* lead a team that year either? Impossible? Think a moment, piece the clues together, and nail him for a double, plus an extra base for deducing how he pulled off this bizarre feat.

AB: 15
Hits: 15
Total Bases: 34
RBI: 15

INNING 9
FALL CLASSICS

1 What Hall of Famer led the Cards with 6 RBI in their 1968 fall defeat to the Tigers? RBI single.

2 The Cards participated in the third post-1900 World Series in which all the games were played in the same park. We won't embarrass anyone by asking who their opponents were. Instead, we want to know how many days the Series took to complete. RBI double.

3 What Cardinal is the only pitcher in World Series history to date to surrender three gopher balls in one inning? The barrage came in his second start that classic, and although he did not figure in the decision, the Cards lost, forcing a seventh game that they would win. But when the Birds repeated as NL champs the next year, our hurler worked just a third of an inning in relief that October and never appeared in the bigs again. RBI double.

4 Who was the only Card to win at least one game in both the 1985 and 1987 Fall Classic? Two-run single.

5 The Cards' top hitter in the 1926 World Series rapped .417 and banged an inside-the-park home run to help win Game 2 for Pete Alexander, 6–2. Who was he and what was especially significant about his round-tripper? You need both for a homer of your own.

6 Just one Card to date has outmaneuvered the opposing defense to steal home in World Series play, and he did it during a Series-clinching seventh game. During the regular season that year he swiped just two bags, no shock considering his position. Single, plus a RBI for the year of his surprise Series theft.

7 Who scored the winning run on either a wild pitch or passed ball—opinions vary—in the final game of the only postseason

World Championship won by a St. Louis ML entry prior to 1926? Triple, plus a ribby for the year it happened.

8 During the 1968 Series he relieved in two games for the Cards, yielding seven hits in four innings, including a homer to Al Kaline. The previous year he had started one fall contest against the Red Sox and lost despite pitching effectively. He'd subsequently drop a Series start with another NL outfit, but by then everyone who played in his first two Fall Classics had already retired. Name him for a RBI double.

9 St. Louis squared off against three different National League clubs in postseason play in the nineteenth century. What is the only one of the three that is no longer in the NL? Single, plus an extra base for the year that club faced the St. Louis AA champs.

10 Two Cards slugged at least one round-tripper in each of the Redbirds' three 1960s Series appearances—1964, 1967, and 1968. Triple for nailing both, just a single for one.

11 Taylor Douthit, the Cards' leadoff hitter and center fielder in the first four games of the 1926 World Series, was unable to play the final three contests. What sub outfielder finished the Series in Douthit's leadoff spot? If we note that he spent his entire seven-year career in Redbirds garb and also saw action in the 1928 Series, can you slide past us for a bases-clearing triple?

12 Acquired for his wheels, he batted leadoff in each game as the Cards suffered an embarrassing Series sweep. His paltry .182 Series BA didn't help matters, and though he led the Birds that season with 26 steals, it was this vet speedster's lone year in the Mound City. Speak his name for a single.

13 The Birds had little to chirp about in the 1928 Fall Classic. For three bags, name the only Cards regular to hit .300 against Yankees pitching in the four-game rout. The lone clue you should need is that this Hall of Famer played the same position as the man who led all Cards hitters in the 1926 affair. RBI for the position.

14 If we tell you the Cards opened the 1926 World Series on the road, can you tell us what day of the week Sportsman's Park hosted its first twentieth-century postseason game? Double.

AB: 14
Hits: 14
Total Bases: 30
RBI: 13

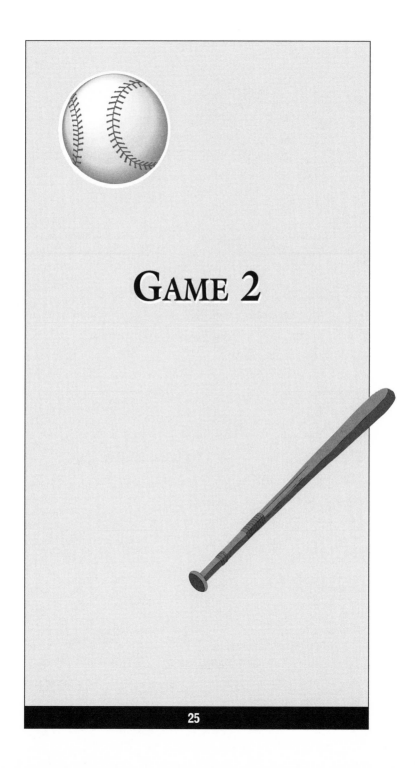

GAME 2

INNING 1
STELLAR STICKWIELDERS

1 Except for 1945 when he was in the military, Stan Musial led the Cards outright in hits in every season from 1943 through 1956. In 1957, however, a swinger in his sophomore season tied Musial with 176 hits and two years later our mystery man slapped 178 more safeties to lead the club solo. This Mississippian was dealt away after turning 27, and despite lasting until 1966, he never really shone again. Two-run double.

2 What slugging first sacker led the first two St. Louis NL entries (1892–1893) in RBI, only to earn a return ticket to the minors for his effort? Even with the clue that he debuted in 1884 with the UA St. Louis Maroons as a pitcher, went 12–1, and again earned naught but a ticket back to the minors, we'll still cough up a two-run triple.

3 The Birds' lone .300-hitting bat-title qualifier in 1991 was a gardener who poked .305 and paced the Cards with 173 hits while making the All-Star team. Acquired the year before for Willie McGee, he was just 27 when the Redbirds dealt him to the Royals after he poked .295 in 131 games. RBI single for this Dominican switch-hitter.

4 After Jesse Burkett fled to the Browns following the 1901 season, the Cards had only one more stickman score as many as 250 total bases in a season prior to the end of the Deadball Era in 1919. His 253 TB remained a post-1900 club record for a player at his position until 1953. The clues are there for experts to triple, and win a RBI for the name of the man who broke his post-1900 team mark for that position.

5 At age 23, he set the Cards season record for total bases by a shortstop with 308 just two years after posting what was then the club's second highest total base figure at short. Single, plus a RBI for the year he established the current team high.

6 Two members of a certain well-known Cards trio were teammates on another ML club in their final seasons as active players, and the third was a teammate of a rookie named Vander Meer in his finale. Since they all quit as active ML players in the same year, they share the distinction of being the first performers with a minimum of 1,000 at bats as a Cardinal to exit the majors after logging a .500+ career slugging average with the Birds. Name the trio for a deuce, plus an extra base for knowing the teams for which all three played in their final seasons. No credit for knowing less than all three.

7 Pop a bloop single for naming the only player who debuted since 1950 to slap 100 or more triples in a Cards uniform.

8 The first batting champ in NL history to play with two different teams the year he reigned began the season with the Cards after being a World Series hero the year before. His name merits a single, plus a ribby for the team that owned him when he wore the crown.

9 It wouldn't be our style if we didn't include some less than stellar stickwielders here. What third sacker set the St. Louis NL club record for the lowest BA (minimum 400 PA) when he stroked all of .191 in 1908? We'll even add that his .223 career BA ranked the lowest of any position player with at least 1,000 at bats as a Card prior to expansion. Turn on the midnight oil for this weak sticker who was born and bred in St. Louis and score a RBI triple once we also note that he played in the 1909 World Series.

10 Excluding strike years, who had the lowest total to lead the Cards in hits in any season since the beginning of the Lively Ball Era? We'll clue you that it happened the year after a Birds flag-winning season, plus that he's in the Hall of Fame, and still stake you to a triple.

11 When Jesse Burkett hit .396 for St. Louis in 1899 after coming west from Cleveland, he was the first Mound City batsman in nine years to top .340. What future Hall of Famer had been the last previous performer to do so when he belted .350 for St. Louis in 1890 and finished as the runner-up for the AA bat crown? RBI double.

12 Subsequent to NL expansion in 1962, who was the first Cards second baseman (minimum 502 PA) to hit .300 twice? After stroking an even .300 to lead the team, he poked .303 the next year with 191 hits, the most in a season by a Birds keystone sacker since Red Schoendienst. Single, plus a RBI for his two-year run.

13 Three Cardinals had seasons in which they batted over .330 (minimum 500 PA) during the decade of the 1950s (1951–1960). One is so easy he merits only a sac hit, but if you nab the other two as well, you can elevate your score to a RBI triple.

14 During the heart of the Deadball Era—from 1905 through 1915—only one bat-title qualifier produced as many as two .300 seasons for the Redbirds. His highwater mark was .314 in 1912 after stroking .302 two years earlier. Many authorities consider him to have been the Cards' best player during his tenure in St. Louis. Double.

15 What member of the Cards franchise set an all-time ML record for the lowest batting average by a league leader in on base percentage when he smote a pitiful .231 for a flag winner but parlayed his 116 walks into a loop-best .400 OBP? Double for him, extra base for the year.

AB: 15
Hits: 15
Total Bases: 32
RBI: 12

INNING 2
TEAM TEASERS

1 Simple logic should steer you to the first Cards crew to blast 200 seat-reachers in a season. They were bolstered by a quartet that belted at least 25 homers apiece, accounting for more than two-thirds of the team's total. Single, plus a RBI for all four sluggers.

2 The Cardinals began as an original member of the American Association in 1882. What are the three other present NL franchises that first breathed life as members of the rebel AA? Need all for a double, single for two, zip for knowing just one.

3 What was the only Cards flag winner to date that hit below .250 as a team? They also tossed a club-record 27 shutouts that season. Historians shouldn't need more than a moment to reason out the year here. Single.

4 The Cards were the last of the eight NL teams that began the 1901 season to win their first pennant in the twentieth century. What was the last of the original AL franchises to win its first flag? RBI single, plus an extra base for the team's breakthrough year.

5 The first St. Louis big league entry to lose as many as 100 games in a season also spun a club-low .221 winning percentage. Nail the year it happened for a triple, plus a RBI for the name of the NL pennant winner that season.

6 The most recent Redbirds entry to sport a trio of .300-hitting outfielders, all of whom were batting-title qualifiers, placed second behind the Bucs in the Eastern Division that season. Double for the year, and a RBI for each of the Cards fly hawks.

7 After finishing fourth in 1901, the Cards did not breathe first-division air again for over a decade. For a home run, nail the breakthrough year when they rose to third, and take an extra RBI for the hurler who led the charge by topping the NL that season in ERA.

8 What new NL team record (since broken by several subsequent senior-loop pennant winners) did the Cardinals set when they copped their first NL flag in 1926? Two-run homer.

9 The most recent Birds squad to average more than one error per game in a season lost 90 contests and was led in miscues by a third sacker who paced the NL at his position with 26. Double for the year, plus two extra bases for their heavy-handed hot-corner man who hit all of .228.

10 The St. Louis NL franchise has never won more than three straight pennants since joining the NL. The exact years the Cards enjoyed their lone three-year reign to date as NL champs is worth only a single.

11 And we'll award another single, plus a ribby, if you know the exact years of the Cards' all-time franchise-record four-year pennant reign when they were still known as the Browns.

12 The Cardinals were the first team in ML history to seat a woman as the team's principal owner. She inherited the club from her uncle, and you can be the proud inheritor of a two-run triple for speaking the name of his favorite niece.

13 In a four-season span once upon a time the Cardinals both won and lost a NL pennant, respectively, on the final day of the regular season. What was the four-year spread and what rival NL team was able to make the reverse claim in that same period? RBI double.

14 The 1906 Cubs romped to the NL pennant with a loop-record 116 wins. How many games did the Cards finish in arrears of the Cubs that season? Utilize the clue that it was only half a game less than the franchise's all-time record for the most games finishing behind the pennant winner, then come within two games of the margin and earn a RBI triple, plus an extra RBI for each team of the two Cards clubs that share that finishing-in-arrears record.

15 Excluding strike years, what Cards team is the last ML club to date that poked fewer than 60 homers in a season? Adding that they rebounded from a sub-.500 season to win the pennant the following campaign downscales this to a double for the year.

AB: 15
Hits: 15
Total Bases: 34
RBI: 17

INNING 3
CY YOUNG SIZZLERS

1 Cy Young would probably not have won his namesake award in either of the two seasons he spent in St. Louis NL livery. In which of the two seasons did he nonetheless post a stellar 26–16 mark for the first St. Louis entry to break .500 since the present pitching distance was established in 1893? Double.

2 Pitchers on flag winners tend to do well in the Cy Young balloting, especially if they pace their league in wins. What Redbird bore Cy Young credentials when he tied for the NL lead in victories with 20 in the year the Cards won their first NL pennant? RBI triple.

3 The most recent Cardinal ERA qualifier to post a figure below 2.00 placed second that year in the Cy Young race, and it proved to be the only time he ever received any votes during his 12-year big-top stay. Single, plus a RBI for his superb season.

4 What hurler unquestionably would have been the Cards' first near unanimous Cy Young winner had the award existed the season he bulldozed the Gas House Gang to the flag? Just a single.

5 His career record of 108–48 with St. Louis teams translates to a .692 winning percentage. In his first full season in the bigs he was 40–13 and led his loop in both wins and ERA with a 2.07 mark. The clues are all there to bag a double for this retroactive Cy Young winner, plus a RBI for his greatest season.

6 What Card placed third in the Cy Young balloting the year he broke the St. Louis NL entry's season record for fewest walks per nine innings (minimum one inning pitched per team game) at 0.77? Truly zeroed in on the black, he issued just 20 free passes in 233 frames that season. RBI single for this soft tosser, an extra ribby for the year, plus two more bases for naming the Hall of Famer who previously held the Redbirds record for free-pass stinginess.

7 Who is the only pitcher among this sextet to garner a Cy Young vote as a Redbird? Steve Carlton, Al Hrabosky, Danny Cox, Bob Forsch, Larry Jackson, Ray Sadecki. RBI single.

8 Two other hurlers in addition to Cy Young have won 25 or more games in a season while pitching for a St. Louis NL entry, and each would probably have won at least one Cy Young trophy during his career had the award then existed. This one's a bit harder than it might seem on the surface, so we'll bestow a RBI double for both names.

9 He led the NL in Ks and placed second in ERA while leading a Cards club that finished 20 games out of first with 14 victories. Arguably, his was one of the best seasons among hurlers who worked on a sub-.500 Birds unit, but he failed to earn a single Cy Young vote and was dealt to the Giants in March of the following year. Double for this slim strikeout king who possessed one of the finest curveballs of his era.

10 In three of his four years with the Cards he earned Cy Young votes but never placed higher than third in the balloting as a Bird. Despite his relatively brief stint in the Mound City, the Birds nonetheless retired his number, perhaps in part because he won Cy Young hardware with another NL club. Single.

11 Name the only hurler in Cards history who conceivably could have won a Cy Young Award after turning 40. He coupled

21 wins with the NL lead among all qualifiers (minimum 154 innings) in fewest baserunners allowed per nine innings in his first full season in a St. Louis suit. Two-bagger for him, plus a RBI for his big year with the Cards.

12 His 24 wins in 1936 were two behind NL leader Carl Hubbell's total. But Hubbell had just three saves whereas he had a loop-leading 11 to make a strong case for top pitching honors that year. RBI single.

13 Who was the only Card to earn Cy Young votes twice during the 1990s (1991–2000)? His votes came in successive seasons, and in the first instance he placed second overall in the NL. During those two campaigns he combined to win 10 games, which should tell you the role he played on the Birds staff. Single, plus a RBI for his two-year run.

14 A lackluster 7–12 rookie year from a certain Cards hurler was followed by a season with a loop-leading 21 wins and .700 winning percentage. But the Cy Young that year went instead to a hurler from the pennant-winning Pirates. His superlative soph season proved to be his most valuable performance as a Card but not the most valuable thing he ever did for the team. Two for him, RBI for the year.

AB: 14
Hits: 14
Total Bases: 24
RBI: 11

INNING 4
BULLPEN BLAZERS

1 The first pitcher in NL history to bag 40+ saves three straight years totaled 133 in 154 chances during that span, all in Redbirds raiment. We can't go more than a single here, but we'll tack on an extra sack if you nail his three-year skein.

2 The first Cardinal to bag as many as 20 saves in a season achieved that mark when he nabbed 26 two years prior to NL expansion. Double.

3 Who is the most recent hurler to top the NL in saves while toiling for a Cards pennant winner? No Birds devotee would expect more than a bloop hit for this one, but we'll add a RBI for the year and an extra base for knowing his save total.

4 Name the Cards slab man who at one stretch in his 10-year career appeared in 77 games over the course of two seasons and posted 12 wins without suffering a loss. We'll add that 73 of those games were in relief and that he twice led the NL in both saves and hill appearances en route to a dazzling 51–20 career record in Birds wear. Two bases for him and an extra base for his two perfect back-to-back 1.000 winning percentage seasons.

5 Who was the first pitcher to exit St. Loo after making as many as 200 hill appearances as a Card without ever starting a game? In his four Redbirds seasons, this southpaw notched 60 saves, leading the club each year in that department. Clueing you that two of those campaigns came with Birds flag winners makes this just a double.

6 The first Cards reliever to appear in 70+ games for three straight seasons, he led the team in saves with 29 the first year and again with 15 the following campaign before being dropped from his closer's role. Across a decade he made over 600 appearances with five NL clubs before exiting the bigs. RBI single, plus an extra base for nailing his three-year relief run in St. Louis.

7 What former AL MVP winner once led the Cards in relief appearances (55) and also tied for the team lead in saves (11)? In parts of three seasons with the Redbirds, he worked nearly 100 games before being dealt during a campaign in which the Birds won it all. Double, plus a RBI for his finest pen season in the Mound City.

8 In his two years in the Cards pen, this chunky lefty totaled a whopping 163 appearances but failed to earn a single save. Tapped for only seven save opportunities during his Redbirds stint, he blew them all before moving to the Rockies in a swap for Aaron Miles and Larry Bigbie. Single, plus a RBI for his two-year workhorse span.

9 Who had the most career saves of any right-hander in Cards history prior to Solly Hemus's first season as the Cards manager? Tough solo homer.

10 In a five-year sojourn, spent exclusively with the Cards, he relieved in over 200 games and once led a Redbirds flag winner with 19 saves. Commentators at the time often noted that this World Series participant was born the same day Don Larsen tossed his Series perfecto against Brooklyn. Double.

11 What Cards 20-game winner tied for the NL lead with five saves in 1928 to accompany his 21 wins? He also paced the senior loop the previous year in saves while winning 17. RBI double.

12 The NL co-leader in saves with the above man in 1928 was not only a Card, but more importantly, the senior loop's stingiest slab man among all hurlers in at least 25 games, allowing just 9.8 opposing hitters to reach base per nine innings in his 27 appearances. Experts will slap their skulls if they don't score a homer here, but others will struggle.

13 A year after becoming the first Cards reliever to drop 10 decisions in a season from the pen, he led the majors in saves as a Bird and tied the then existing season save record. Single for him, plus a RBI for pegging the two seasons in question.

14 What pre-expansion bullpenner held the Cards season save record by a southpaw prior to 1965 and still holds a share of the team's career lefty saves record with 60? RBI double.

AB: 14
Hits: 14
Total Bases: 31
RBI: 9

INNING 5
WHO'D THEY COME UP WITH?

Credit yourself with two extra RBI if you not only know the team with which each of the following Cardinals debuted but can also state the year.

1 Lonnie Smith. Single.

2 Estel Crabtree. Triple.

3 Buster Adams. Two-run triple.

4 John Tudor. Single.

5 Frankie Frisch. RBI single.

6 Joaquin Andujar. Single.

7 Tip O'Neill. Two-run double.

8 Ron Taylor. We'll go a round-tripper here.

9 Eddie Stanky. Two-run single.

10 Pete Vuckovich. Two-run triple.

11 Ron Northey. Bloop double.

12 Jose Oquendo. RBI single.

13 Arlie Latham. Grand slam even if you know just the team, and a gold star if you also know the year.

14 Danny Litwhiler. Two-bagger.

15 Bob Tewksbury. RBI single.

    AB: 15
    Hits: 15
    Total Bases: 30
    RBI: 46

INNING 6
FAMOUS FEATS

1 What Cardinal is the only pitcher in ML history to toss five consecutive shutouts against one team in a season? This lefty's mercurial mastery of the defending World Champion Dodgers helped him to an 11–5 slate and accounted for all of his whitewashings that campaign. Three years later, while toiling for the Expos against the Redbirds, he achieved a second one-of-a-kind feat when he threw the first ML pitch in Canada. Double.

2 When Jim Bottomley delivered his record 12 RBI game against Brooklyn on September 16, 1924, whose old single-game ribbies mark did he break? All you should need for a RBI single is our clue that the former record holder, to his chagrin, witnessed the event.

3 What Cardinal won the 1950 All-Star Game at Chicago's Comiskey Park with a solo shot leading off the 14th inning to give the NL squad a 4–3 verdict? He's worth a single, plus an extra base if you know from which side of the plate he batted when he went deep after learning the hurler he faced threw with the same arm as Vinegar Bend Mizell. Plus three RBI if you know the Tigers chucker whom he victimized.

4 In his debut season, this Redbird rapped .429 in just six games and smote homers in each of his first two ML at bats to become the initial player ever to do so in the senior circuit. After going hitless in two at bats the following year, he vanished from the bigs. True, Taguchi hails from Japan, but this Famous Feat achiever was actually the first Nippon native to play for the Cards. Single, plus a RBI for the year he made NL history.

5 What Redbird is now recognized to have been the first Triple Crown winner in National League history? Twenty-some years ago he was considered only to have been the third to do so, but Hugh Duffy's 1894 season and Heinie Zimmerman's 1912 season have since been discovered not to have been Triple Crown accomplishments. He's worth a single; his breakthrough year rates a RBI.

6 What Card not long ago became the first NL pitcher ever to hit into an unassisted triple play in regular season action? No palooka with the stick that year, this right-hander stroked 17 hits and even homered for La Russa's squad. Take a single for him, a RBI for the year, and an extra base for knowing the Dominican shortstop who tripled him up.

7 On the morning of May 24, 1909, Christy Mathewson was riding a 24-game winning streak against the Cards—the all-time record for the most consecutive wins against one club. That afternoon, at the Polo Grounds, his skein was broken when he lost 3–1 to a hurler who was otherwise among the most luckless in ML history. The twirler began his ML career at the tender age of 18 as primarily a first baseman with the Phillies in 1904 and finished with the 1910 Cards when he was still just 24 years old after the Birds decided they could live without him despite his having led the club in wins, winning percentage, and ERA. Utilize our lavish clues to smack a solo homer.

8 After the current pitching distance was set in 1893, who was the first performer on a St. Louis NL club to draw more walks than games played (minimum 100 contests) in a season? He led the senior loop in free passes that season, plus OBP and slugging while making the All-Star team. RBI single, plus an extra base for the year.

9 What Card held the NL record for the most consecutive games played (895) for the better part of 14 seasons? The previous mark of 822 had belonged to a Pirate, and the Cards stalwart saw his record fall to a Cub who was later eclipsed by Steve Garvey. The Card's worth a single, plus an extra base if you know both the Pirate whose mark he broke and the Cub who later assumed his mantle.

10 The first batsman in NL history to rap as many as 250 hits in a season was a Cardinal. His name and the year he did it are worth only a single. But two RBI are yours if you know whose NL record he broke that year after we generously tell you the previous record holder spent three seasons in a St. Louis NL suit.

11 Who was the youngest player to drill a homer for the Cards franchise? Just 18 at the time, he hit his second home run later that season but did not go deep again for nearly five years. His initial blast came against Reds reliever Frank Smith, who teamed with this switch-hitter on the Birds two years later. Unlike many teenagers who swiftly slipped from the scene, our man stuck for 19 seasons despite carrying a .227 career BA. Double, plus a RBI for the year of his precocious feat.

12 What Cardinals stickman missed becoming the most recent NL Triple Crown winner one year by a margin of just one home run? RBI single, but only if you know both the man and the year.

13 The first ML player to slug as many as four pinch homers in a season in two consecutive years did it with the Cards en route to hitting 14 career pinch blasts to set a new big league record (since broken). Exiting as a Redbird at age 40, he debuted in pro ball with the New York Black Yankees of the Negro National League. RBI double for this Indiana bammer.

14 There have been five Triple Crowns in ML history that were achieved by players in a loop other than the American League. Four of the five belong to members of the Cards franchise. Name the two performers who claimed one Triple Crown each in St. Louis garb and the player who bagged two such honors and claim a RBI single, plus two extra bases if you know all four of the seasons involved.

15 Say hello to this Cards righty who made fewer than 10 starts one season but nonetheless became the most recent senior-loop pitcher to win two complete games in one day. Mostly employed as a Birds bullpen operative across parts of five Mound City seasons, he later did World Series relief duty with both the Birds and the Giants. These clues should ring your chimes for a triple, plus a RBI for the year.

AB: 15
Hits: 15
Total Bases: 29
RBI: 16

INNING 7
MEMORABLE MONIKERS

Here are some memorable nicknames in Cards lore. To what Bird does each refer?

1 Eck. Single.

2 Frenchy. Double.

3 Country. Snap single.

4 Spittin' Bill. Double.

5 The Mad Hungarian. Single.

6 Slats. RBI double.

7 Arlie. RBI single.

8 Four Sack. Two-bagger.

9 Bake. Single.

10 Peanuts. Single.

11 Snags. Home run.

12 The Wizard of Oz. Single.

13 Showboat. Two-run triple.

14 Cupid. RBI double.

15 Mighty Mite. Three bases.

> **AB:** 15
> **Hits:** 15
> **Total Bases:** 27
> **RBI:** 6

INNING 8
FORGOTTEN
UNFORGETTABLES

All of these performers lurk, at the very least, on the fringes of the consciousness of every Cards fan who harbors illusions that he or she thoroughly knows the Birds' history. But each did something so noteworthy that all baseball mavens should be able to claim a nodding acquaintance with him.

1 Upon arriving from the AL, he made his first start in Birds threads a memorable one by tossing a complete-game one-hitter against the Mets. Two years later he tied for the Cards team lead with 15 wins while topping all club qualifiers with a 3.26 ERA. But two seasons after that, elbow woes limited him to a 2–5 coda at age 26. RBI single for remembering this Dominican right-hander.

2 Acquired by the Cards after smashing 23 homers with 101 ribbies for San Diego of the PCL in 1953, this slugging first sacker debuted on Opening Day 1954. Although he appeared in just 91 games over four years hitting .246, he should forever be remembered as the first African American to don a Redbirds uniform. RBI double.

3 In nine years up top, this portly righty toiled for eight clubs, winning only 46 games while losing 49. Just once did he reach double figures in victories and that came when he exploded for an 18–7 log for one of La Russa's crews. Not fooling the Birds, however, he found himself swapped in March of the following year and immediately reverted to his losing ways over the next two seasons before departing from the show. Single, plus a RBI for his one unforgettable year in the Mound City.

4 He collected 627 at bats as a Cards rookie, hit .287, and played every game at second base in Series action that fall. Never again—largely because he ran afoul of Commissioner Happy Chandler—did he log more than 146 AB in a season. Tough two-run three-bagger for the New Orleans native who finished his career with the first Philadelphia A's team that was managed by someone other than Connie Mack. We'll toss in an extra ribby for knowing his final ML season.

5 An Ohio native who cut his teeth with the 1915 Portsmouth, Ohio State League champs, he first joined the Cards in 1918 and left the club midway through the 1922 season with an inoperable brain tumor and a .302 career batting average, including a high of .350 in 1921. RBI two-bagger for this slim gardener whose time in the show was so tragically cut short.

6 In his finest season by far, he began 8–0 and finished at 16–9 for a Cards club that saw postseason action. Regrettably, elbow tendonitis eventually led to rotator cuff surgery, shelving him the following year. Upon his return, he posted a 9–18 composite over his last two seasons before the Birds reluctantly gave up on him. RBI single, plus an extra ribby for the year.

7 Prior to the twenty-first century, only one batsman in Cards franchise history rapped .300 or better (minimum of 400 AB) in his lone season with the Birds. We'll clue you that he did it as a teammate of a Hall of Famer who stroked a nifty .344 in his sole year as a Cardinal, albeit in just 334 at bats. We'll also note that in his five seasons as a regular, ending with the 1903 Phils, his lowest BA—.300 on the nose—came in the year he manned the keystone sack for St. Loo. Homer for him, plus another RBI for his Hall of Fame teammate, and a bonus ribby for the year they teamed up on the Cards for just that one season.

8 What performer in by far his most productive season as a Card played at least 15 games at each of the three outfield positions and posted a .942 OPS and a .341 BA at age 38, only to never play another game in the field for the Redbirds? We'll add the clue that his last name appeared twice on every envelope that was addressed to him or his family when he was a child, toss in a second clue that he finished with the 1944 Reds at age 41, and still award a circuit clout.

9 How quickly we forget the lone Card still short of age 20 to qualify for an ERA crown since the mound was set at its present 60'6" distance. And how quickly we should remember after learning that at age 23 he won 20 for the first Cards team to see Series action without either Jim Bottomley, Frankie Frisch, or Stan Musial in its lineup. Two bags for him, one for the year he won 20.

10 In 1951 the Cards took two vaunted pitchers of Slavic descent to spring training. Both made the club, and each won seven games in his frosh year and gave promise of big things ahead. But, alas, neither ever delivered on his early promise, finishing with just 25 and 31 career wins, respectively. For a RBI triple, name the two highly touted arms, one of Czech ancestry and one of Croatian, after digesting the final clue that both their last names began with P.

11 Across parts of eight seasons in the show, he kicked around with five clubs and produced 22 homers in 717 career at bats. A bush league masher, he pounded over 200 seat-reachers, including a minor-league-leading 42 taters with Denver of the American

Association in 1976. With the Cards the following year, he continued to tear the cover off the ball, stroking 33 hits in 83 at bats for a searing .398 BA, plus a 1.090 OPS, earning a ticket to sit on the Birds bench for two more seasons before exiting the bigs. Double if you recall his unforgettable super-sub season.

12 The first outfielder since 1900 to total as many as 350 plate appearances for three straight seasons (1961–1963) while walking fewer than 15 times each year was this impatient Cards pastureman who hailed from St. Louis. Dubbed "Stan Musial's Caddy," he'll take you to third.

13 Lest we forget, the lone slab man in Cards history to bag 20 wins in the only season he won so much as a single game in Birds livery was 23–13 after being blasted in his first St. Louis appearance the previous year. He skipped to the AL Browns in 1902 but later returned to the NL to match his season high of 23 wins with another senior-loop team that wore red and white. Triple for him, RBI for his other NL team.

14 In his first ML decision he beat Brooklyn at Ebbets Field, 7–6. Five days later he blanked the Dodgers in Sportsman's Park, 2–0. After topping the Phils to bring his record to 3–0, he bested the front-running Braves and their ace Warren Spahn, 4–2. Now 4–0, he seemed headed for the Rookie of the Year Award. But, alas, arm trouble shut him down after a 5–2 loss to Cincinnati on September 2 to reduce his record to 7–5, and he never won another game in the majors. RBI single for this never-to-be-forgotten righty, plus an extra base for the year he both soared and crashed in the space of less than three months.

AB: 14
Hits: 14
Total Bases: 34
RBI: 15

INNING 9
PEERLESS PILOTS

1 Name the only man to date who can claim he managed the Cards to a pennant and won a NL bat crown as a member of the Braves franchise. Triple.

2 Who is the only former ML catcher to manage a Cards flag winner? Your clue is that he once tried to catch something that was even harder to handle than Walter Johnson—a ball dropped from the top of the Washington Monument. RBI double.

3 Plucked from the Cards coaching lines to pilot the Birds after Fred Hutchinson's late-season departure, he had served as their archrival Cubs' regular skipper for three seasons earlier that decade after starring with the Bruins for years. Name him for a double.

4 Who sat at the Cards helm for three full seasons and finished more than 50 games behind the NL flag winner in each of them? Solo homer, plus two bonus RBI for his three-year stretch in baseball hell.

5 The Redbirds have a tradition of plucking managers from within their flock of former players. This performer logged the most career games of any Cardinal before WWII who *never* piloted them. In fact, he had appeared in more Birds box scores than anyone other than Hornsby at that time. However, he did skipper in the Mound City, but with the Cards' cross-town rivals, supplanting the Rajah at the Browns helm. RBI single.

6 What ML umpire renowned for his pugnacious temperament sat at the controls of a St. Louis NL team for a full season while he was still in the midst of his officiating career? The club finished a very bad last, but you'll finish with a very good two-run triple for his name, plus two extra ribbies for the year.

7 Which one of the following longtime baseball men piloted a St. Louis entry in two different major leagues but never managed a St. Louis team in the NL? John McGraw, Branch Rickey, Jack Hendricks, Fielder Jones, Chris Von der Ahe, Charlie Comiskey, Lee Fohl. Double.

8 Who piloted the Cards in Enos Slaughter's last season in Redbirds flannels? RBI single, plus a second ribby for the year.

9 Less than a decade after playing in a World Series with the Cardinals, he managed the Birds to a second-place finish in his only full season as a ML helmsman. Cut through the clues here, for the prize is high. Home run.

10 Who were the only two men prior to Frankie Frisch to pilot a Redbirds NL entry for as long as five seasons? One was a player-manager and both men are in the Hall of Fame. RBI double, but you need both.

11 In 1980 no fewer than four men tried their hand unsuccessfully at the Cards wheel. Three of them are among the most well-known names in team lore: Ken Boyer, Whitey Herzog, and Red Schoendienst. Name the fourth man, a longtime Cards coach who was earning his second try as an interim manager of the club. Home run.

12 Who piloted the first St. Louis NL entry to finish in the first division (upper half of the league)? He was a player-manager who came of age in St. Louis's Goose Hill area. Three bags for him, two RBI for the year.

13 The most recent man to manage the Cards for a full season despite never playing in the majors is worth a solid two-base knock.

14 Who was the Cards' most recent player-manager to date? Two bags for him and one for his last year as an active player with the Cards.

AB: 14
Hits: 14
Total Bases: 36
RBI: 16

GAME 3

INNING 1
SHELL-SHOCKED SLINGERS

1 He led the NL by surrendering 35 homers while logging the worst ERA (6.02) that year among senior-loop qualifiers, all for a Cards world champ. Held in complete disregard by season's end, he was left off the NLCS and World Series rosters to avert further damage. Single, plus a gift RBI for the year.

2 His .211 winning percentage as a starter-reliever is the lowest in Cards franchise history among chuckers who logged a minimum of 150 innings in a season, as he closed at 4–15. Just 22 at the time, he made a 180-degree turn the following campaign, going 14–5 and upping his winning percentage by more than .500 points to .737. Exiting the majors with the Orioles 11 years later, he finished at 129–112. RBI double, plus an extra base for his shell-shocked year.

3 He surrendered a Cards franchise record 238 earned runs the season after he captured a NL ERA crown. Nevertheless, he won 27 games in his shell-shocked campaign, and you'll shock all your compadres when you rattle off his name for a two-bagger, plus a RBI for his record-setting 238 season.

4 In 17 starts a certain Cards hurler posted a 7.14 ERA, allowed 15.81 baserunners per nine, and made fans shudder when opposing batters pummeled him at a .324 clip. Like many others you'll encounter in this chapter, he was no bum. In fact, before his unexpected meltdown, he was the only ML pitcher to bag as many as 15 victories in each of the previous five seasons. Single, plus a gift RBI for the year.

5 What Birds southpaw slinger yielded 135 runs in just 237⅓ innings, yet posted a neat 15–9 record that season? Of course, it didn't hurt that he was chucking for a pennant winner in his first full season as a ML starter. RBI double, plus an extra base for his year of generosity.

6 Won-lost records can be deceiving, and this performer's slate is a good example. Look beyond his 14–14 ledger and you'll notice that the Cards won 90 games that year and his 4.78 ERA was just a hundredth of a point behind the worst among all ML qualifiers. In addition, he led the bigs in baserunners allowed per nine at 14.67. But this St. Louis native had plenty of fine years to come, just not in the Mound City. Two for the lefty the Birds let slip through their nest.

7 Who is the lone Cards twirler to face as many as 1,300 batters in a season since the close of the Deadball Era in 1919? He did it twice, no less, but all you need for a two-bagger is his name and one of the years he toed the rubber against so many opponent sticks.

8 Who is the only Cards lefty since the end of the Deadball Era to experience a season in which he lost as many as 15 games and logged a sub-.500 record while posting an ERA below 3.00? That year he went 13–15 with a 2.51 ERA before going 9–4 the following campaign on a Redbirds world champ. Double, plus a RBI for his luckless losing season.

9 In 1895 this redheaded righty saw a Cards club-record 17.4 baserunners on the average reach base against his slants in every nine innings he pitched. Not surprisingly he logged a dismal 6–19 record in his only season in St. Loo garb, but five years earlier he went 25–14 for a flag bearer. Home run for his name, two extra RBI for his pennant-winning team.

10 Pitchers with 5.00+ ERAs seldom survived more than a season or two in the Deadball Era. But the Cards had two such hurlers in 1913 and both had careers lasting at least six seasons. One was a rookie who was 6–14 with a 5.15 ERA; the other was a soph twirler with a 10–22 mark accompanying his 5.08 ERA. The rook later fashioned a neat 1.88 ERA for the flag-winning Giants in 1917 while the soph logged a fine 2.51 ERA in his junior year before doing a slow fade to the minors. The name of either of these shell-shocked hurlers will net a two-bagger; two-run homer if you nail both.

11 Who is the only Cards pitcher since 1900 to log at least 100 innings in two consecutive seasons and post an ERA above 5.00 in both campaigns? Rather amazingly, in neither year did this journeyman lefty post a losing record as he went a combined 17–16 with a 5.09 ERA before moving to the BoSox during the latter season. RBI single, plus an extra sack for his two-year run.

12 In 1895 a certain St. Loo hurler was plastered for a 5.22 ERA while winning just six games. Some 59 years later a veteran chucker with the same last name went 7–13 and was rocked to the tune of a 5.26 ERA in his last of eight seasons with the Cards. The 1895 slinger never pitched another inning in the majors after earlier posting four 20-win seasons. But the later-day Card led the AL in hill appearances five years afterward as a member of a flag winner. You need the first names of both for a three-baser. Sac hit if you know only the twentieth-century tosser, plus a RBI for his AL pennant winner.

13 Among all Cards who logged as many as 200 innings in a season since 1900, his 5.28 ERA is the worst in club history, and to further dampen that season he yielded 35 homers, at the time the most by a Redbirds chucker in more than half a century. Along the way he also surrendered more hits per nine (11.19) than any other NL qualifier that year. Still he managed a 13–9 slate in his lone season at Busch. RBI single, plus an extra base for the year.

14 What reclusive right-hander led the NL in winning percentage as a member of a Cards flag winner and followed two years later by surrendering a club-record 39 home runs? The season he was shelled for 39 jacks marked the end of his first tour of duty with the Birds, but he returned to the team eight years later and won 13 at age 40. Two-bagger, plus an extra base for his shell-shocked season.

15 After losing 24 games as a rookie, he really came unraveled in his sophomore year, dropping a Cards franchise record 35 games.

We'll tell you his 35 defeats are also a post-1892 ML season record and still award a two-run double, plus an extra base for his horrendous year.

AB: 15
Hits: 15
Total Bases: 37
RBI: 15

INNING 2
HOME RUN KINGS

1 Just two Cards in the franchise's long history, reaching all the way back to 1882, have won as many as two straight loop home run crowns. Double for both, zip for less.

2 Who was the first Cardinals fly hawk since NL expansion in 1962 to cream as many as 20 homers as an outfielder in two separate campaigns? The man you seek pounded 22 and 20, respectively, on the last two Cards clubs Whitey Herzog guided for a full term. RBI single, plus an extra base for the years in question.

3 After Johnny Mize was traded to the Giants prior to the 1942 season, Stan Musial took over the throne as the Redbirds slugging king. Between Mize's departure and NL expansion in 1962, Musial went deep 443 times. During that span only two other batsmen hit as many as 100 jacks in Cards threads. You need both for a RBI single and are favored by us with the clue that the pair were never teammates on the Cards or any other ML club.

4 Although Mark McGwire didn't play in his first game with the Cards until August 1, 1997, he still placed second on the team in homers that year with 24. Who paced the 1997 Redbirds with 31 four-baggers? Single.

5 Which of these ball hawks hit the most career home runs in a Cards suit? Wally Moon, Terry Moore, George Watkins, Tip O'Neill, Rip Repulski, Ray Blades. Two-bagger.

6 Who led the Cards with 30 homers despite missing 40 games during La Russa's first season as Birds skipper? It was also this Texas thumper's freshman year in Redbirds flannels after he signed as a free agent that winter. At the time he may have sported the game's biggest biceps. Paste a RBI single.

7 Only three sluggers in ML history can claim seasons in which they hit .400 and hammered as many as 20 home runs. Name the Card who could boast that he did it not just once but three times in his career. Single.

8 Who was the only performer in Cards franchise history prior to Bob Gibson to hit as many as 10 career home runs while serving as a pitcher? Even though he's a 200-game winner, we'll still cede a RBI double.

9 For a double, name the only performer to pace the Cards in four-baggers under the dugout command of both Johnny Keane and Red Schoendienst.

10 The first Cardinal to go homerless for an entire season in 600 or more at bats did it in 1920 and still holds the club record for the most AB in a homerless season with 639. Not a weak hitter by any means, he rapped 204 safeties that year and batted .319. Name this third sacker for a solo homer.

11 The year Big Mac launched 65 missiles, this performer quietly broke Ken Boyer's season mark for homers by a Cards third baseman. In the process, he also placed second on the team with 34 taters. Single for him with the added info that Albert never hit that many in a season while playing the hot corner.

12 Since the Cards joined the NL in 1892, only one performer—pitchers included—has collected as many as 1,000 at bats with the Birds without ever hitting a home run. He batted .268 during his stint in St. Louis but had just a .319 slugging average. His lone big league dinger came with the 1948 Cubs, two years after he left St. Louis. A Series performer as a Cards rookie, he rates a RBI triple.

13 The first home run king in Cards franchise history reigned the year of the franchise's inception. His seven home runs topped the American Association in 1882 but were not enough to earn him an encore appearance in the Mound City. Last seen with the 1885 Baltimore AA club, he shares a surname with one of the Cards' 1946 Series heroes. The last name alone brings a sac hit, but it's worth a homer of your own if you know his first name, too.

14 Apart from Ted Simmons, historically the Cards have not sported much power behind the plate. In 1962, for the first time, they featured two receivers who both reached double figures in four-baggers. The lefty half of the platoon hailed from Shick-shinny, Pa., and later served as Texas League president from 1976 until his death in 1991. The righty swinger was dealt to the Braves during the 1963 season with Bob Sadowski for a fading Lew Burdette. Triple for both, single for one.

15 Who holds the Cards club record for the most taters among sluggers who played just one year in Redbirds raiment? Dealt to the Dodgers just days after the regular season concluded, he poled 34 seat-rattlers in the Mound City despite missing 40 games and even made the All-Star squad. RBI single, plus an extra base for the year.

AB: 15
Hits: 15
Total Bases: 31
RBI: 8

INNING 3
MASTER MOUNDSMEN

1 The first southpaw to notch a 20-win season in a St. Louis ML suit bagged no less than 24 victories to go with a 3.69 ERA. It was his only full campaign for a Mound City entry, and it also proved to be his big league coda despite winning 114 games in little over five seasons in a career abbreviated by drink and debauchery. Hop from the shore to the closest lily pad and bang a triple, plus a ribby for his final season.

2 What post-expansion hillman won 19 games for a Cards pennant winner but only logged enough innings to qualify for an ERA crown in two of his six seasons as a Redbird? Telling you that the Birds posted the lowest NL team ERA since 1920 the year he won 19 should help aficionados zero in on the season. Single for him.

3 He never won 20 for the Cards or anyone else, but he once had a three-year string with the Birds in which he won 19, 17, and then 18. Triple for this longtime Cards mainstay who was an All-Star selection in both leagues and posted 134 career wins between 1947 and 1961.

4 Stroke a bloop double by naming the only hillman in Cards history to post as many as 25 saves for a club that won fewer than 60 games. A bit of thought will lead you to just about the only possible season in which this one-of-a-kind feat occurred.

5 When Dizzy Dean rang up 30 wins in 1934, whose post-1900 club season record for victories did he break? Double for the hurler, plus an extra base for his win total and another for his big season with the Birds.

---

6 Mark McGwire's slugging heroics in 1998 distracted many a fan from the hard fact that the Cards finished 19 games out of first. Their top winner that year was this journeyman lefty who notched just 11 victories with a bloated 5.07 ERA. RBI single.

7 In his 10-year career, all of it spent with the Cardinals, he made just 117 starts but collected 97 wins. He is the most recent hurler to throw a shutout and lead the NL in saves in the same season. What's more, he is the lone performer in ML history whose first name is also the first letter of the Greek alphabet. Enough clues here to ring up a ground-ruled double.

8 What Cardinal holds the current ML record for the most relief appearances during a 20-win season? Solly Hemus employed him in 52 games, including 28 from the pen, as this righty became the first NLer in history to bag 20 victories without completing at least 10 starts. Double.

9 This one is an easy seat-reacher for experts. Who is the only hurler to start as many as 20 games during his time with the Cards and complete every contest he started? Need we add that he could still make that claim if the total were upped to 50 games?

10 Who posted the highest season ERA to date of any Cards 20-game winner since 1900? This 6'5" curveballer went 20–9 with a 3.91 ERA in his first year in Busch after recording a 6.61 ERA in 32 starts with his previous outfit. Single, plus a RBI for the year.

11 The first hurler to win 20 games twice for a NL franchise based in St. Louis finished with more career doubles (216) than wins (138). Do we really need to add that he compiled nearly 2,000 hits in the majors? Tough enough to go for a solo homer, plus an extra ribby if you know his two 20-game seasons with St. Louis.

12 The first Cards lefty subsequent to NL expansion in 1962 to bag 15+ wins in consecutive seasons actually bagged his first big league victory years before at age 18 with another NL club and retired after 20 campaigns with a 193–183 slate. RBI single, plus an extra base for his two-year Redbirds win skein.

13 The 1902 Cards set records for both the most decisions and the most innings logged by rookie hurlers. The lone returnee from the 1901 rotation won 10 games in each of the first two years in the twentieth century and only four thereafter. Even with the clue that he, a current film comedian, and an outfielder who played on three AL pennant winners in the 1910s share the same first and last name, this is still on the board as a homer.

14 Believed (incorrectly) until the early 2000s to have been only 18 when he won 25 games for the first edition of the Cards franchise, he followed with 28 victories in 1883 and 24 the next year. Sitting on 77 wins after his first three ML seasons and supposedly still just 20 years old, he won only 25 more games in the show before succumbing to wing woes. A really big homer awaits you if you name him.

15 When Mort Cooper allowed just 9.04 enemy baserunners per nine innings in 1942, whose post-1892 (the last year the pitching distance was still just 50 feet) Cards club record did he break for the fewest baserunners per nine innings by an ERA qualifier? Be careful here if you want to score a double—the name belongs to a Hall of Famer and he set the mark in his only full season as a Card.

AB: 15
Hits: 15
Total Bases: 39
RBI: 10

INNING 4
NO-HIT NUGGETS

1 Who is the most recent hurler in Cards franchise history to spin a no-hitter on a Birds pennant winner? All but the last of his 10-year career was spent in Redbirds threads, and the season he entered the charmed hitless circle was his best, as he went 14–8 with a nifty 2.26 ERA. Of course his mound performance was particularly special, being the first of its kind. Single for him, a RBI for the year, but add an extra base for knowing why his feat was so sweet.

2 St. Louis is home to two of the only three major league teams to date that have had a pitcher twirl a regulation-length no-hit game in his first big-show start. Name both hurlers for a homer, single for knowing only one. An extra ribby for the chucker whose debut no-no came with a team that did not represent St. Louis.

3 *What?* St. Louis has showcased yet a third pitcher who tossed a no-no in his maiden ML start? It's a fact, and what's more, the hurler was the first in ML history to accomplish it. His gem came with the AA Browns on September 23, 1890, at St. Louis and resulted in a 21–2 win over Philadelphia that saw him give up nine walks. Why has his feat been buried over the years? Because the game was shortened to seven innings, in part because it was so one-sided, and hence isn't recognized as a no-no by MLB. He was nicknamed "Kid" in honor of another rookie pitcher that season who had a much more prominent career, and your name is in lights for the three-run homer you'll bang by nailing him.

4 Would you believe that only one Cards catcher to date has called signals for two nine-inning no-nos? The games came seven seasons apart during his 13-year stay at Busch, but you're headed for the bush leagues if you don't nail this star receiver. RBI single.

THE ULTIMATE ST. LOUIS CARDINALS BASEBALL CHALLENGE

5 The first NL no-hit game to take place in Sportsman's Park was tailored by a Hall of Fame hurler on July 17, 1924. If we share the tidbit that Casey Stengel played for the team he faced that day, can you name both the hurler and his opponents for a two-run double?

6 Who tossed a no-hitter for the Cards during a season in which he compiled a deplorable 5–14 slate with a hair-raising 5.85 ERA? Dealt by the Birds after that campaign, he was immediately converted to the pen by another NL outfit and twice made over 70 appearances in relief. Single, plus a RBI for the year.

7 Who was the first slab man to throw a no-hitter as a member of a Cards flag winner? We'll add that it came in the second game of a doubleheader against Brooklyn and the Dodgers made only three hits that day. RBI single.

8 The sole lefty to spin a no-hitter for the St. Louis NL entry since 1892 bagged just seven career wins, all with the Redbirds, and earned only one after his no-no. Adding that his hitless performance came during his rookie season and that it represented his only career complete game scales this down to a single, but grab a RBI for the year he showcased no-hit stuff.

9 Although the Cards franchise has featured many fine hurlers, only one of them to date has fashioned two no-hitters in Birds threads. His no-nos came five years apart and in both seasons he posted losing records. In between his hitless performances, his older brother spun a ML no-hitter as well. Single for the Bird, plus a RBI for his elder sib.

10 This Redbird had made the NL All-Star team in 1941 and seemed a certainty to win 200 games when he no-hit Cincinnati on August 30 that year. But he finished in 1945, still eight wins short of 200, back with the NL team that had first put his hummer on display 15 years earlier. RBI double, plus an extra base for the ML team that was both his first and last.

11 The first St. Louis NL entry to fall prey to a no-hit hurler featured the loop batting leader that year. He and his eight Birds teammates were collared by a Giants rookie 20-game winner. Name the bat titlist, the no-hit hurler, and the year for three bases. No credit for less than all three answers.

12 Which one of these Cards receivers never caught a no-hitter in Redbirds raiment? Bill DeLancey, Walker Cooper, Darrell Porter, Johnny Edwards, Tim McCarver, Alberto Castillo, Eli Marrero. RBI single.

13 This Redbird fired the first no-hitter at Three Rivers Stadium in an 11–0 trouncing of the Bucs, fanning Willie Stargell to seal the deal. Single.

14 Stan Musial appeared in only one no-hit game during his long career. It came in 1960 and Musial's Cards were the victims, but it's not in the cards for you to score a three-bagger if you can't name the Cubbie that shut down The Man and all his fellow Birds without a hit.

AB: 14
Hits: 14
Total Bases: 28
RBI: 14

INNING 5
WHAT WAS THEIR REAL HANDLE?

1 Chick Hafey. Just a RBI single.

2 Woody Williams. Two-run single.

3 Jake Flowers. Two-run triple.

4 Bruce Sutter. Double.

5 Pickles Dillhoefer. Solo homer.

6 Tip O'Neill. RBI double.

7 Tuck Turner. Two-run triple.

8 Eli Marrero. RBI single.

9 Peanuts Lowrey. Two-run single.

10 Tito Landrum. RBI double.

11 Sparky Adams. Three-run double.

12 Toad Ramsey. Three-run triple.

13 Jumbo McGinnis. Two-run homer.

14 Buster Adams. Grand-slam homer.

15 Bob Gibson. Double.

AB: 15
Hits: 15
Total Bases: 35
RBI: 25

INNING 6
CIRCLING THE GLOBE

1 The Cards are the first ML franchise to showcase an Australian-born performer who collected as many as 2,000 at bats in their livery. A second baseman by trade during his playing days, he later became an undertaker and operated a funeral parlor in the Mound City. RBI triple for this transplanted Aussie who debuted as a first baseman with the 1884 UA champion St. Louis Maroons.

2 This infielder was the first Colombian native to play 1,000 big league games and twice rapped over .300 as a Cards regular. A member of a Redbirds flag winner, he's worth one base.

3 The Cards' most famous Canadian-born player starred in St. Louis before the club joined the NL. His .344 career BA ranks third all-time among performers who collected a minimum of 1,000 at bats in Cards franchise garb. RBI single.

4 What Cuban-born backstopper served three separate stints with the Cards and was a teammate of both Tommy Long and Ducky Medwick? Homer.

5 The first Venezuelan-born performer to play 200 games in Redbirds garb sported a last name that might make some think he hailed from Egypt. Tried everywhere with the Cards but center field and the mound, he'll net you a single.

6 In his lone year with St. Louis, this German-born righty started the game in which Wilbert Robinson made a record seven hits and a then record 11 RBI. Prior to his arrival in the Mound City, he had won 140 games, mostly with Detroit, in a career dating back to 1884. Two-run homer for the pitching half of the original "Pretzels" battery that featured him and catcher Charlie Ganzel.

7 Acquired from the Astros, this infielder hit just .167 in the five games in which Schoendienst employed him in 1973. He remains the only ML player who was born in Okinawa since it became an independent nation. Name him and rap one over the fence for a well-deserved homer.

8 Looking for a grand salami? Fly to Austria, the birthplace of this Bird who briefly nested with the Cards in 1949 and 1951 and in between won 17 with Columbus of the American Association in 1950. Sadly, he died in the Mound City at age 43.

9 Probably the smallest regular performer in St. Louis team history was this 5'4" Scottish gardener. Born in Campsie, Scotland, he was a key member of the first two major league flag winners that represented St. Louis. RBI triple.

10 As a regular gardener with the 1983 Cards, he hit .284 and swiped 34 sacks before shifting to first base a year later when George Hendrick returned to the pasture. Two years earlier he had been the first Nicaraguan to play in a World Series for a NL entry. Single.

11 You'll need to rack your mind to conjure up the name of the Cards infielder in the early part of the twentieth century who was a native of Hereford, England. Later in his career he won a home run crown with another NL team despite hitting zero four-baggers that season on the road. Rates a four-bagger of your own.

12 After bagging 56 wins in six Redbird seasons this Northampton, England, native blew out his elbow, shelving him for two years. Never returning to the Mound City, he drifted indifferently through three teams across five seasons before retiring. RBI single.

13 The last decisions of this 17-year big leaguer came in Cards threads as he exited after the 1972 season with 589 games under his belt. He's the only major leaguer born in Poland, so tap a slow-roller and stop at first.

14 What Aruban-born hurler toiled on a Cards world champ? Dealt away before the season ended, this stocky righty posted an uninspiring 5.24 ERA and allowed over 15 baserunners per nine innings in Birds wear. Single, plus a charitable RBI for the year.

15 Tony Mullane is the best all-around player who hailed from Ireland to grace the Cards franchise record books, but a certain player-manager and outfielder ranks a not-too-distant second. In his four seasons with the Cards, he played with both Cy Young and Three Finger Brown. RBI double.

AB: 15
Hits: 15
Total Bases: 35
RBI: 15

STELLAR STICKWIELDERS

1 Counting only performers who had a minimum of 2,000 at bats with the Cardinals after they joined the NL in 1892, who had the highest career on base percentage as a Bird prior to Rogers Hornsby's arrival? He's a Hall of Famer, but you won't be if you whiff on this RBI double.

2 The Cards nearly strung together four straight NL pennants from 1942 through 1945. Responsible in large part was Stan Musial, who hit .341 during that span. Among all team members who collected at least 1,500 PA over that four-year stretch, which one stood second to Stan with a .289 mark? We'll offer the clues that he began the skein in 1942 by hitting .258 in 95 games, slipped to a dismal .224 the following year, and still finished his career in 1952 with a solid .296 BA. For a double, snare this forgotten 1946 All-Star who paced all NL outfielders in fielding average in 1944 and five years later banged .340 in 106 games with the Pirates, most of them served at first base.

3 Which of these pre-expansion Birds ranks the highest on the club's list of career leaders in on base percentage (minimum 2,000 PA)? Solly Hemus, Chick Hafey, Enos Slaughter, Ray Blades, Joe Medwick, Wally Moon, Frankie Frisch. RBI double.

4 In his rookie year he replaced an injured fellow fledgling midway through the season and hit just .267 but had a fine .380 on base percentage. As a soph, he raised his OBP to .421 when he walked 90 times and scored 92 runs in 115 games. Because he never again played enough to qualify for a batting title, his soph OBP mark stands as the all-time record for the highest OBP by a performer who had only one ML season in which he was a bat-title qualifier. A third sacker by trade, he also played some outfield and second base and finished with the 1953 Phils. Home run for this forgotten Card who compiled the highest OBP to date (minimum 500 PA) by a St. Louis NL third sacker as a soph—yes, even higher than Albert—and fared so poorly thereafter.

5 When Leo Durocher plummeted to a ML worst .203 BA in 1937, he was the first Cards batting-title qualifier since 1919 to fall below .230. Name the lowly .223 hitter in 1919 who was one of the Cards' offensive leaders during most of his other seasons with the club. Three-bagger.

6 Prior to Tim McCarver's arrival, who held the Cards all-time season record for the most total bases by a catcher? Careful—it may not be who you think, but the receiver who set the mark nonetheless received due recognition for his achievement. RBI double.

7 When Rogers Hornsby logged a .484 slugging average in 1917, he set a new Cards franchise record for the highest SA by a shortstop. Hornsby's mark still holds today. And today it's worth a two-run homer if you know whose club mark Hornsby broke, plus a third RBI for the year the old standard was set.

8 In the six-year span between 1920 and 1925, Rogers Hornsby hit .397. Three other Cards with at least 1,000 plate appearances during that period hit .315 or better. One was Jim Bottomley, whose career BA rested at a cool .350 after his first four seasons in the majors. A second was the ill-fated Austin McHenry, who stood at exactly .315 for that span before exiting so abruptly. The third was an often forgotten Card who put in three years with the club and left with a .317 career BA for his work with the Birds. Earlier in his career he had led the AL in slugging average, and after leaving the Cards he once topped the NL in home runs. Take three if you know his name.

9 What second sacker hit just .213 for a St. Louis NL club but logged a fine .400 OBP? The reason: that year he set a ML season record for the most walks (136) that lasted until 1911. It'll be a crime if you don't smack a RBI triple here, plus a second RBI for the year he did it.

10 In 1953 first sacker Steve Bilko became the first Cardinal to fan 100 times in a season when he logged 125 Ks. Previous to that the club season record for the most whiffs belonged to a rookie infielder who fanned 90 times in 1940 but nonetheless hit a solid .287 in 129 games. It was his lone year as a Cardinal, and never again did he play regularly in the majors. Later, however, he was a longtime San Francisco Giants PR man, which was only logical since he was born and died in San Francisco. Last seen in the majors with the 1945 White Sox, he's your potential grand slam in this category.

11 Currently the Cards franchise has 10 members who posted career BAs of .325 or better with a minimum of 1,500 plate appearances in St. Louis garb. One of the 10 recorded a .790 career OPS as a Card that is more than 100 points below the figure of any of the other nine members of the list. The primary reason? He collected only 73 walks in 1,551 plate appearances with the club. His free-pass nadir came in 1901 when he walked just 21 times while hitting .339 in 502 at bats. Snag a two-run homer if you know the gardener who quit the game after the 1904 season at age 28 to go into the family business and was enticed out of retirement near the end of the 1908 season by the St. Louis Browns, who were making a desperate bid for the AL pennant, only to prove of no help.

12 Among all Cards franchise members who played a minimum of 100 games at third base and logged at least 500 plate appearances in the same season, which of them is the lone figure prior to the end of the Deadball Era in 1919 to post an OPS as high as .780? Now, don't say McGraw, who had only 447 PA in 1900. Or Arlie Latham, whose best Mound City OPS was .779. Rather, it was the man who held the ML record for the highest career OPS (.849) among all retired performers who played a minimum of 1,000 games at third base until Al Rosen left the majors in 1956. At present our man still ranks eighth on that select list, just behind Wade Boggs. Is he a Hall of Famer? Never will be, in part because he was never on a pennant winner in his 13-year career, and we'll gamble a trey that all too many of you have never even heard of him.

13 Who is the only performer since 1900 to swipe as many as 150 bases and compile a .300+ career BA in Cards livery? Two-bagger.

14 This is another conundrum designed to separate our experts from the rest of the flock. Subsequent to 1892, when the Cards first joined the NL, Rogers Hornsby was both the first to collect 2,000 and 3,000 career total bases as a Bird. Spout the name of the first batsman to accumulate 1,000 career total bases in his time with the St. Louis NL franchise and win a three-run homer.

15 Besides Honus Wagner, who is the only other NL shortstop since 1900 to bat at least .330 while plating 100 runs? Naturally, the man you seek is a Card, and his average dropped over 40 points the following season before the Birds waved goodbye to his services. Single, plus a RBI for his standout season.

AB: 15
Hits: 15
Total Bases: 43
RBI: 19

INNING 8
RBI RULERS

1 While leading the NL one year in hits, he also set the Cards season mark for singles by a 100 RBI man. In addition, he topped the NL in ribbies that campaign, besting the Bucs' Willie Stargell by 12. Single, plus a RBI for the year.

2 The Cards' post-1900 season record holder for the most RBI by a pitcher hit .234 the year he knocked home 21 mates, and that figure just about matched his career BA for his seven seasons with the Birds. His relatively short stay should steer you off the knee-jerk answer who happens to rank second with 20 RBI in his best season as a Card. Double for the record holder, plus a generous RBI for his runner-up.

3 For five straight seasons he paced the Cards in RBI with totals ranging from 61 to 109, and one of those leadership years came with a world champ. For a good stretch he was the Redbirds' main slugger in a speed-driven lineup. RBI single, plus an extra base for his five-year reign.

4 Stan Musial not surprisingly holds the record for the most 100 RBI seasons as a Card. How many 100-ribby seasons did Stan have? Double, but down to a sac hit if you come within one.

5 What short-lived Cards sensation was the first hot-corner occupant in ML history to knock home 100 runs in each of his first two seasons in the show? He finished with only 438 career ribbies after debuting with 112 and following with 104 as a soph. RBI double for this rapper whose .268 BA as a rookie remains the lowest to date by a Card enjoying a 100 RBI season.

6 A double awaits if you can name the only performer to date to collect 1,000+ RBI as a Cardinal accompanied by a career BA below .300 for his time with the Birds. In 11 years in St. Loo, he waited until his penultimate season with the Cards to play on his lone flag winner. RBI single.

7 Who had a Cards club-record six straight 100 RBI seasons but never achieved another 100-ribby campaign for the Redbirds or anybody else in his 17-year career? Double, plus two RBI if you know his six-year skein.

8 Between 1981 and 1997, just one Card placed as high as second in the NL RBI race. A first sacker at the time, he totaled 117 ribbies, eight behind the leader, Kevin Mitchell. Single for this man who retired with more career runners plated than Mitchell.

9 Prior to NL expansion in 1962, the Cards received 51 100-RBI seasons. Which of the following Cards is the only one missing from that lengthy list? Les Bell, Austin McHenry, Frankie Frisch,

Buster Adams, George Watkins, Del Ennis, Charlie Comiskey. Two-bagger.

10 The 1908 season was the Cards' post-1900 nadir. Not only did they finish last and lose 105 games, but they also scored only 372 runs, the lowest total of any club since 1900 in a nonstrike year. The club RBI leader that season knocked home just 62 mates. Given the clue that he also led the Cards in homers and was traded over the winter, you should ring up a three-bagger here.

11 When Ozzie Smith drove home his 606th baserunner for the Cards, whose club record did he break for the most career RBI by a shortstop? Knowing that he held many other team shortstop records prior to Ozzie puts you in the driver's seat for a RBI single.

12 Rogers Hornsby plated 1,072 baserunners while a Card, nearly 400 more than the total of the previous club career RBI record holder. Who was he, with a modest total of 689? We'll announce up front that it isn't Tip O'Neill and that our man owns the lowest career OBP of any Cardinal who posted as many as 1,000 at bats at the same position he occupied. Solo homer.

13 What Negro league veteran punched home 29 RBI with eight home runs and a .301 BA in just 103 at bats in 1959? You can brag all you like if you nail this two-run dinger.

14 Not until past the midpoint of the twentieth century did the Cards feature a slugger who cranked as many as 30 homers in a season with fewer than 100 ribbies. His 32 dingers that year were a personal high, but twice later in his career he topped 100 RBI and once even led the NL in ribbies with 119. RBI single.

AB: 14
Hits: 14
Total Bases: 28
RBI: 12

INNING 9
RED-HOT ROOKIES

1 No Cards hurler with at least one inning pitched per team game played averaged more than a strikeout per frame until this frosh arrived and eclipsed Dizzy Dean's club freshman whiff mark. Along the way he topped all ML yearling qualifiers in ERA, starts, and innings. Few realize that his unique surname is an anagram of the unique surname of a Hall of Famer who spent his entire career with one club and once opposed the Cards in Series play. The chucker's a single, plus a RBI for the year. But add an extra base for deciphering the Famer after our last clue that both of their surnames to date are one of a kind in big league annals.

2 He had tough shoes to fill when he replaced Hall of Famer Jake Beckley at the Cards' initial sack midway through the 1907 season, but at the end of the campaign he sported the club's top OPS, albeit a rather modest .673. Our added tip that he remained the Cards' chief offensive force until he jumped to the Federal League in 1914 marks this down to a standup double.

3 During his official rookie year, this Card tied for the NL frosh lead in losses and finished with a sub-.500 record. Lousy debut, right? Others viewed those numbers differently and awarded him that year's NL Rookie of the Year trophy. Of course it didn't hurt that he set a rookie mark (since broken) in a certain department. Piece the clues together for a single, add a RBI for the year, and an extra base for knowing what frosh record he formerly held.

4 Forgotten due to our previous man's exploits, this 24-year-old frosh lefty won 11 games in the Cards rotation that same season and even started a Series contest for the Birds a year later. Nonetheless he closed his career with the 1992 Phillies, the owner of just 28 career victories. Rescue him from oblivion with a RBI single.

5 Prior to Stan Musial's rookie year, who was the only member of the Cards franchise to lead the club in wins and strikeouts and see postseason action, all in his official frosh season? Triple, plus a ribby for his majestic frosh year.

6 He didn't debut until July 18 of his rookie season, but this switch-swinger made his time count as he belted .324 in 262 at bats and became the first Redbird since 1900 to steal at least 20 bases in fewer than 70 games. Finishing with the 1998 Royals, he once bagged a NL MVP, but not with the Birds. Single, plus a RBI for his freshman year.

7 As a Cards rookie, he fanned just 14 times in 146 games and played in the only World Series that never left St. Louis. His soph season saw him play 155 games and be named to the NL All-Star team, but he missed the game because of an injury. His junior year he was traded to the Phils to open a new spot in the lineup for Red Schoendienst. This rook is worth a solo homer; his first three years in the bigs will earn a gift bonus RBI.

8 Unveiled in 1952, a certain lefty led NL rooks in starts, innings, and Ks and also shared the league lead, rookie or no, with 103 walks. The possessor of one of the most colorful nicknames of his era, this Southerner's good for a RBI double.

9 In addition to showcasing almost an entire rookie pitching staff in 1902, the Cards had the NL's top freshman position player. A lefty-hitting center fielder with a smooth stroke, he slapped a neat .311 and followed with three more excellent seasons in St. Louis before burning out early in 1906 at age 28. Two-run homer.

10 Verging on age 30, this Cards rookie posted a nifty 1.53 ERA and 8–2 record as a combination starter-reliever in 1943. It was a role he was to occupy for his entire 10-year career, all of it served in Birds livery. Name this lanky southpaw who finished with the 1954 club. RBI double.

11 When he first joined the Cards late in 1956, after his .350 BA with Omaha led the American Association, this stocky Virginian seemed a lock to be the club's center fielder for the next 10 years and a potential Rookie of the Year candidate in 1957. Alas, while playing winter ball in Central America, he perished in a plane crash before the year was out. Two-run homer.

12 The Cards spring training camp in 1946 was flooded with returning service vets. Nevertheless three players who had rookie status according to today's rules made the club. Two of them were Nippy Jones and Erv Dusak. The third was a 20-year-old Mound City native who became the youngest man in franchise history to catch in as many as 50 games in a season. Name him for a RBI double.

13 His initial ML start late one season produced the first pitching feat of its kind in big league history. The following year, in his official rookie campaign, he led the Cards franchise in walks, with 148. His soph season generated a NL ERA crown, and he celebrated his junior year by winning 27 games and working 441⅓ innings. If you're bright enough to figure out whom we're describing, snare a two-run double.

14 At one point in their history, the Cards featured a different rookie center fielder in three consecutive years. Was that because the first two flopped as frosh? Far from it. Two of the trio bagged NL Rookie of the Year honors and the third hit 68 homers in his four seasons with the Birds, all of them spent as a regular gardener. The trio's worth a double, plus an extra base for this unparalleled three-year string in ML annals of outstanding rookie center fielders.

AB: 14
Hits: 14
Total Bases: 34
RBI: 16

GAME 4

JACK OF ALL TRADES

1 The Birds did everything they could to keep his potent stick in the lineup, playing him at first, third, and both corner outfield positions during his freshman year alone. This All-Star continued to bounce around the field for the next two years before settling at first. Perhaps the easiest single in this book.

2 He saw regular duty at second, third, and short with the Cards, played second in his lone fall appearance with the Birds, and finished with the 1946 Pirates. He was born in Jamesville, N.C., and you can say "Home, James" after banking a solo tater for his name.

3 Although he served as a third sacker on two straight Cards flag winners, he had previously guarded the pasture on an earlier Birds pennant bearer. Enormously popular in the Mound City, he had his playing career ended prematurely by a kidney ailment. RBI single.

4 An easy single is yours for naming the lone Cardinal to win NL batting titles while serving at four different positions.

5 Who is the only man to be able to claim he caught as many as 100 games for the Cards and also won a batting title in a Birds monkeysuit? RBI single, but only if you know both the player and his position when he won the bat crown.

6 A career .296 hitter, he played in five World Series, including three straight with the Cards during his 14-year big league ride. In 1942 he played first in every game of that season's classic and two years later served as the Birds' regular center fielder in October action. Jump all over these clues for a RBI double.

7 The Cards employed him as their primary catcher before shifting his services to third, where he stayed as their hot-corner regular for four years. The following campaign, he worked solely at first before moving to the Cubs in June of that season. In 16 years of big-top action, this well-traveled stick whacked 253 homers. Single.

8 In his four-year career, all spent with the Cards, this lifetime St. Louis resident did duty at every position on the diamond. He began primarily as a third baseman, finished as mainly a backstopper, and played his most games in a season at any one position in 1907 when he was stationed at second in 73 contests. A big hole is shot in your trivia expert rating if you whiff on this two-run homer.

9 He broke in as a shortstop, played third in his first full season in the bigs, and came to the Mound City in 1885 as an all-around handyman. The following year he dropped anchor at second base, which became his primary position in the majors, albeit he played every spot on the diamond at least once in his 10-year career that featured three seasons as a loop leader in walks and one as an OBP champ. RBI triple.

10 Signed as a shortstop, he came up to the Cards as a second baseman, and after two years as a regular at the keystone sack, he switched to third. Along the way he led the NL in fielding at both positions while providing steady stick work before closing his 16-year sojourn with the 1992 Angels. RBI single.

11 You can count on the fingers of one hand the performers who have converted to serving as position players after enjoying at least one double-figure-win season as pitchers since the mound was set at its present distance in 1893. Who are the only two St. Louis NL performers since the rubber was set at 60'6" to post a double-figure-win season in Mound City threads and later have at least one season in which they collected as many as 150 at bats while serving solely as a position player? One is a routine single, but nail the other as well and up your earnings to a two-run homer.

12 Slick leather work kept him in the Cards middle infield for eight seasons, but his stick was truly for the birds as he posted a woeful .616 OPS in over 2,000 PA in the Mound City before moving to the Cubs for Donnie Moore. Deliver a knock-out blow by recalling the first performer who was never a teammate of Austin McHenry to log 300+ games as a Redbird at both second and short. Double.

13 In his 13-year-career, all spent with the Cards, he was a regular at three different positions and even tried his hand at pitching a bit. He never played so much as a single inning at first base, second base, shortstop, or catcher. Salt away a RBI two-bagger.

14 He appeared in nearly 1,200 games, with more than half of them coming at second. But Whitey Herzog played him everywhere one year, including a four-inning relief stint against the Braves in which our man unhappily absorbed the loss in a 19-inning marathon. Single, plus a RBI for the year.

15 He was a fixture at a certain infield position in all but one of his 11 seasons with the Cards. The lone exception was 1957, when he paced the NL in fielding at his interim position that year. The player's worth two, his regular position rates an extra base, and his interim position can boost you to a home run if you nail all three answers.

AB: 15
Hits: 15
Total Bases: 32
RBI: 13

INNING 2
MEMORABLE MONIKERS

Name the Cards sporting these monikers.

1 El Gato. RBI single.

2 Spike. Homer.

3 Tripp. Single.

4 Cowboy or Bronco. Grand-slam homer.

5 Pol. Triple.

6 Stubby. Single.

7 The Hat. Two-bagger.

8 Sleeper. Three-run homer.

9 Sunny Jim. RBI single.

10 Dots. Triple.

11 Possum. Two-run triple.

12 Wild Bill. RBI single.

13 Rebel. Solo homer.

14 Pink. Homer.

15 Fiddler. RBI triple.

> **AB:** 15
> **Hits:** 15
> **Total Bases:** 39
> **RBI:** 16

INNING 3
TUMULTUOUS TRADES

1 Just weeks after Bing Devine became the Cards GM in late 1957, he made his first deal, shipping pitchers Marty Kutyna and Ted Wieand to the Reds for outfielder Joe Taylor, plus this key performer who would play on three Cards pennant winners. RBI single.

2 In 1908 the Cards were dreadful for the third season in a row. In the desperate hope of sparking renewed fan interest, team brass traded for Roger Bresnahan of the Giants in December 1908 and named him player-manager. By then Bresnahan was on the down slope as a player—he never again logged 100 games in a season after his acquisition. The three players the Cards surrendered for him were a serviceable catcher named Admiral Schlei, plus a hurler who won 18 games in 1909 and the 1909 NL home run king. Name the pitcher and homer champ in this one-sided trade and claim a two-run triple. Single if you know only one.

3 The Cards acquired a vital cog in one of their eventual World Championship teams by dealing a former 20-game winner for a hitter who was only a year away from having a MVP season. Double, but you need both players in this straight-up swap to score.

4 In the winter of 1981, the Cards obtained Steve Mura and Alan Olmstead from the Padres in exchange for Sixto Lezcano and Luis DeLeon. Keen-eyed readers will have spotted that we omitted the two key players in this mega-deal, one who went to the Birds and the other to the Pads. They occupied the same position on the diamond, and you can occupy first base, but you need to name them both or else go back to the bench empty handed.

5 Branch Rickey believed in trading a player while he was still at his peak so that he would bring full value, but sometimes he miscalculated badly. What two Cards stars did Rickey unload to the Dodgers in June 1940 for the likes of Sam Nahem, Ernie Koy, Carl Doyle, Bert Haas, and $125,000? The clue that both had hit over .330 in 1939 but only one of them was a position player shaves this to a triple for both and a sac hit for just one.

6 We won't insult you by asking whom the Cards acquired from the Cubs on June 15, 1964, along with pitchers Jack Spring and Paul Toth. However, you can score a triple in your ledger for recalling the trio the Birds flew to Wrigley in exchange for Mr. Brock. Single for anything less.

7 What future three-time .300 hitter did the Birds receive in a straight-up swap for righty Eric Rasmussen? A potent stick on a Redbirds World Champion, he made two All-Star teams in the Mound City. Single.

8 In May of 1947 the Cards swapped pitcher Freddie Schmidt and future bat titlist Harry Walker to the Phils for a slugger who, alas, was never more than a part-time gardener in St. Louis. He's worth a two-run homer.

9 The Cards took a big gamble when they dumped Joe Garagiola, Howie Pollet, Ted Wilks, Bill Howerton, and Dick Cole in June 1951 to acquire two Pirates stalwarts. One, pitcher Cliff Chambers, won just 18 games in his three seasons with the Cards, but the other was even more disappointing. Expected to be the perfect complement to Musial and Slaughter, he was gone in less than a year, the owner of a sub-.250 BA in his brief stint as a Card. RBI double even after we add that this gardener later partially revived his career with Cleveland.

10 Branch Rickey made more good trades than bad ones for the Cards. One of his best brought a Hall of Fame hurler west from the Boston Braves in June 1930 for journeyman chucker Fred Frankhouse and aging Bill Sherdel. Name the Famer who was a heavy contributor to the 1930 and 1931 flag winners and add a RBI double to your stats.

11 What Cooperstown hillman came to St. Louis from Chicago in midseason one year for naught but the waiver price and not only helped the Cards win a World Championship but also later had a 20-win season as a Bird? You should need no more to score a single.

12 Judging that Ripper Collins was about to begin slipping, Branch Rickey dealt him to the Cubs after the 1936 season along with pitcher Roy Parmelee and earned nothing but praise from Cards fans when the hurler he acquired won 83 games in St. Louis before being returned to the Cubs after the 1942 season was under way. Two-bagger.

13 Bing Devine made many fine decisions in the front office, but a persuasive argument can be mounted that from June 1971 through April 1972 he engineered some of the worst deals ever by one GM in that short a span. Over those 11 months, in four separate deals, Devine unloaded a quartet of hurlers who would win over 700 games after exiting St. Louis while getting painfully little in return. During that stretch he also squandered a future six-time .300-hitting outfielder in yet another swap. Tally a triple for naming all four chuckers, a double for three, and just a single for anything less. Add an extra base for the pastureman Devine also so foolishly discarded.

14 In 1919 Lee Meadows became the only hurler in NL history to date to suffer double-digit loss totals with two different teams in the same season when he dropped 10 for the Cards before being dealt to the Phils, where he lost the same number by season's end. Meadows proved to have a lot of gas left in his arm, but the player who accompanied him to the Phils in return for three players who had all departed the Cards by 1920 was soon to be banned permanently from the game. Name this slim first sacker who moved his gear from Sportsman's Park to Robison Field in 1917 after being acquired from the Browns. Solo home run.

15 The Yanks were bilked big-time in October 1981, sending a man to the Cards who would rap over 2,200 hits in 18 seasons up top. He's a check-swing single, but add two extra bases for recalling the Redbirds lefty the Bombers acquired who never again threw another pitch in the majors.

AB: 15
Hits: 15
Total Bases: 36
RBI: 9

INNING 4
TEAM TEASERS

1 The last Cards club to date to sport two 20-game winners grabbed the pennant. Although both were still in their early thirties, neither came close to those victory totals in any subsequent season. Snag a single for the year and a RBI for each of their 20-win twirlers.

2 The Cards have never won 100 games in a season without claiming either a pennant or a division title. What Birds club came the closest to cracking the 100-win barrier while achieving no more than also-ran status? The only clue you should need to stroke a two-run double is that the Cardinals featured a rookie with the one-of-a-kind nickname "Subway Sam" that same season. Add two extra bases for Sam's last name.

3 The most recent Cards entry to lose as many as 100 games in back-to-back seasons was the 1907–1908 crew. Who is the lone Hall of Famer to play so much as a single inning for the Birds in either of those seasons? The clue that he wrapped up a 20-year ML career with the 1907 team should win you a trip around the bases for a solo homer.

4 Just once during the decade of the 1950s (1951–1960) did the Cardinals find themselves playing meaningful games as late as mid-September. Score a RBI double for the year the Birds dreamed of a fall date with Casey Stengel's Yankees before fading to second place and finishing eight games out of the hunt.

5 The last NL club to date to boast three 200-hit men was this Cards team that placed second in the junior loop that year with 93 wins while leading the league in batting, runs, doubles, triples, OBP, and hits. Double for the year, plus one RBI apiece for each 200-hit maker.

6 A two-run homer is yours if you know the last season that the AL Browns finished with a better winning percentage than the NL Cardinals. Your clues are that both clubs finished fourth that year in their respective leagues and no teams based in New York appeared in the World Series.

7 This Cards club came within one game of winning a World Championship with no pitcher on the staff bagging more than 11 victories and without a single ERA-title qualifier under 3.50. Grab a single for the year. Add two bases for naming their trio of 11-game winners, but back to just a single for anything less than all three.

8 What Cardinals team was led in hits by the later-banned Gene Paulette (126), with Cliff Heathcote third on the club (90), Mike Gonzalez fourth (88), and Doug Baird and Bob Fisher tied for fifth (78)? The year is worth three, provided you also know the Hall of Famer who finished second to Paulette with 117 safeties and also paced the club in every extra base hit department.

9 The most recent Cards team to post an ERA below 3.00 was also the first Redbirds squad to fan 1,000 batters. Although they allowed the fewest runs in the NL, the offense plated the third lowest total in the loop, contributing to their finishing 13 games behind the division leader. RBI single.

10 Even including strike years, this Cards club hit the fewest homers in a season by a flag winner since the 1920s. How weak were they in the power department? No fewer than six regulars failed to reach double figures that year, and Mark McGwire blasted more seat-reachers in 1998 than the entire Redbirds squad you seek. RBI single for the year.

11 As play began on August 9 of a particular season, this Cards entrant trailed the Dodgers by 12 games, but thereafter the Birds clawed the NL, going 39–10 before edging the Cubs at the wire by two games and swooping into the Series. Single for the season this miracle comeback occurred.

12 The first Redbirds team to bag more saves than complete games notched over 100 victories and won it all that season. Take a single for the year and an extra base for knowing their complete-game leader with 12.

13 The 1908 Cards did not sport a single Hall of Famer on their roster all year. Many seasons would pass before the next Redbirds club could make the same unhappy claim, but one of their skippers that year later made Cooperstown. Double for the year and a RBI for the pilot.

14 What Cards squad was the first in NL history to win 100+ games in a season without featuring a single 20-game winner? Still, their top victory man tied for the senior loop lead with 19 on a Redbirds world champ. Double for the year, plus two ribbies for naming their win leader.

15 What post-1900 Cards unit finished in the second division despite boasting two 20-game winners? In addition, they spun a post-1900-record 146 complete games but placed fifth in the NL, more than 30 games behind McGraw's Giants. Double for the season, plus three RBI for naming their two 20-game winners.

AB: 15
Hits: 15
Total Bases: 34
RBI: 19

INNING 5
BRAZEN BASE THIEVES

1 Lou Brock won his third successive NL theft title in 1968, but he wasn't the first Card to bag three NL steal crowns. Who was? Double.

2 Between 1966 and 1974, Lou Brock led the NL in steals every year but one. The man who snapped his string and bested him by six swipes spent his first four big league seasons in Redbirds threads as Brock's teammate. Name him for a RBI single.

3 The first St. Louis performer to claim a share of a NL stolen base crown tied for top honors in 1900 with New York's George Van Haltren. It was his first of four seasons in the Mound City, and in each he hit over .300 en route to a .301 career BA and more than 2,000 hits over 17 campaigns. Don't be a sap and go wrong here. Three-bagger.

4 Name the first Card to top the NL in steals outright after winning a theft crown earlier in his career with another NL team. He rates just a single, plus a RBI for his former club.

5 This Redbird nabbed 28 bases in 52 tries and in so doing set the post-1920 officially documented record for the worst season success rate (.538) by a player who made more than 50 attempts. We'll help you along by mentioning that a year later he became the first Card except Lou Brock to lead the club in steals since Brock's arrival in St. Loo. Single, plus a RBI for nailing both years.

6 In parts of 10 seasons with the Birds, he snatched over 150 bases but snagged as many as 30 only once. However, that year he drove opposing receivers mad, totaling 31 in just 34 attempts for a nifty .912 success rate. The Cards won the pennant that season, and you can win a double by supplying this infielder's name, plus a RBI for the year.

7 What Hall of Famer led the NL in thefts as a rookie with the Cards but never won another steals crown and finished a 19-year career with only 89 swipes? Two-bagger for him, plus a RBI for his rookie year.

8 Prior to Lou Brock, only one performer had notched as many as 200 career steals as a member of the NL Cardinals. His personal high of 32 came in 1923 when he was enjoying his fourth consecutive .300+ season while serving in the Birds garden. Even with all that info, we're still anteing up a solo homer.

9 What Cardinal holds the post-1900 ML season record for the most steals by a player who hit under .250 that year? For a while this weak stick received far more ink than his overall talent deserved due to his wheels, but it took 13 years and six rueful teams to realize it. Single.

10 The rules for what constituted a stolen base were much more liberal in the 1880s. Still, no other first sacker in ML history has ever pilfered anywhere near the 117 a certain St. Louis gateway guardian garnered in 1887. Double.

11 His 99 career thefts in Cards garb lead all Redbirds at his position since 1900. Double for this one-time NL batting champ, plus a RBI for nailing his spot on the diamond.

12 What future NL home run king (alas, in another senior-loop uniform) set a post-1900 Cards season theft record of 48 in 1908 that was later tied but never broken until Lou Brock appeared in St. Loo? Triple.

13 Even prior to 1898, when stolen bases were credited much more freely than nowadays, no Cards catcher has ever swiped as many as 20 bases in a season. Who set the post-1897 club receivers' record with 18 thefts in 1913? Two years later he was dealt to Cincinnati, where he played for 13 seasons. RBI triple.

14 Who set a Cards season negative club record when he played 159 games and failed to steal a single base? It was his first year in the Mound City and he arrived in an even-up swap for the future

Hall of Famer he supplanted that season at first. Single for the slowpoke, a RBI for the year, plus an extra base for the Cooperstown performer the Cards sent packing.

15 Who is the only Cardinal to claim a batting crown in a year in which he failed to steal any bases? Tough two-run single.

AB: 15
Hits: 15
Total Bases: 30
RBI: 11

INNING 6
MOMENTS TO REMEMBER

1 On April 23, 1999, a certain Redbird became the first player to power two grand slams in one inning, but what made his Moment to Remember even more unique is that both blasts came off the same pitcher. The swatter's an easy single for Cards fans, but you can go for two by naming his mound victim.

2 The first position player in ML history to appear on the field wearing glasses was a Card, and his "shining" Moment to Remember, on April 13, 1921, resulted in his nickname. Three-bagger.

3 His Moment to Remember came on September 11, 1974, when the Cards beat the Mets 4–3 in a marathon 25-inning game. The winning pitcher, he bagged what proved to be his eighth and last victory for the Mound City crew during his only season in Redbirds raiment. No flash in the pan, this Missourian departed the show a year later with 140 career wins, most of them in the AL. Double for this righty whose given name was Wilfred.

4 This Redbird's first Moment to Remember came when he belted a homer from both sides of the plate in the same game. Those two blasts accounted for one-third of his season total. Never a big bammer, he popped just 89 taters in over 8,000 career at bats. RBI single, plus an extra base for the year he became the first Redbird to go deep both ways.

5 What Redbirds freshman experienced two Moments to Remember when he homered on the first pitch he ever saw in the bigs and later that same season retired the last batter in the World Series? Single.

6 Cards fans received a bizarre Moment to Remember in 1935 when they discovered that their 32-year-old rookie hurler was born in a Pennsylvania town with the same name as the last name of one of his catchers in his frosh season. No common surname this one; the backstopper is the only performer in ML history to bear it, and the same can be said for the pitcher's last name. Triple for the hurler; stretch it to a homer if you also know the catcher's name, but just a sac hit for the catcher alone.

7 What Card pounded three homers in one game but was rewarded for his Moment to Remember by being sent packing the following month for Joe Ferguson and two lesser lights? RBI single, plus an extra base for the year.

8 Frank Woodward won only three games for the Cardinals, but his third and final win came in a home game against the Pirates on September 28, 1919, that marked the last day of the NL season. What made Woodward's win forever memorable in Cards lore? Two-run triple.

9 By today's rules he was still officially a rookie when he stepped to the plate on June 3, 1902, against Boston's Togie Pittinger as a pinch hitter for Cards pitcher Ed Murphy. The sacks were jammed, two were out, the Cards trailed 8–5, and Pittinger quickly got our yearling down in the count 0-and-2. But the frosh the *Boston Globe* deemed "a light-looking left-hander" then took Pittinger's next pitch deep to right field, over the head of

Boston gardener Pat Carney, and into the stands, to put his team ahead 9–8. Later research determined that our rook had just hit the first pinch grand slam in ML history, and research even farther down the road credited him with a save for having remained in the game to ice the Birds win in the bottom of the ninth. No mere flash in the pan, the heroic lefty went on to lead the 1902 Cards both in victories (16) and the highest batting average (.319) among all players with a minimum of 100 at bats. Two-run triple if you can put a name to the perpetrator of this Cards famous Moment to Remember.

10 On August 6, 1949, the Cards had a runner on and their cleanup hitter up with two out in the first frame against a Giants lefty who was just returning to the majors after being banned for some four years. The Cards batter rocketed a pitch into the bleachers for an apparent two-run homer, only to discover as he started around the bases that the lefty had balked before delivering the gopher ball. As per the rules of that time, the runs were canceled. The cleanup hitter then flied out to end the inning and the Cards, robbed of his two-run homer, dropped the game 3–1 and later lost the NL pennant by a one-game margin. It remains one of the most infamous Moments to Remember in Birds history, but you can gain instant fame and a three-run homer by naming both the Cards cleanup hitter and the Giant who escaped with a victory in a game that proved vital to St. Louis's pennant hopes by committing not just one balk but three such gaffes. Down to a double if you know just one of the principals.

11 The game in the nation's capital on July 25, 1892, matched two teams going nowhere that year in the NL race: Washington and St. Louis. Washington struck quickly, tallying four runs in the first, but St. Louis's 35-year-old pitcher then buckled down and held the Senators scoreless the remainder of the game while his mates tattooed Washington pitchers for seven runs. That 7–4 verdict proved to be this Mound City native's last of 365 career wins, a ML record at the time. His first triumph had come some 17 years earlier, also in a St. Louis uniform, when he beat Keokuk

3–2 in a contest played at a neutral site in Burlington, New Jersey. It, too, was a Moment to Remember in that no other ML 300-game winner has collected his initial victory in the Garden State. Name him and score a two-bagger here.

12 He played nearly 1,000 games in the majors as an outfielder, but his most memorable moments came on the occasions when he sprang off the bench to pinch hit. The last such moment in 1953 came with the Cardinals and resulted in his 22nd pinch safety of the season, tying the then existing ML season record. No fluke feat was his, for the previous year he had gone 13-for-27 in pinch roles. RBI double.

13 In 1922 the Rajah rolled out a Redbirds record 33-game hitting streak. His skein was halted by a star performer who would later win 30 games combined for two consecutive Cards flag winners. Score yourself a double for this streak-stopping future Card's Moment to Remember.

14 You'll get no more than a safe dribbler down the third base line by naming the Card whose Moment to Remember occurred when he became the only player in ML history to slam four homers and plate 12 mates in the same game. Add a RBI for the year he did it.

> **AB:** 14
> **Hits:** 14
> **Total Bases:** 33
> **RBI:** 12

INNING 7
PEERLESS PILOTS

1 Who is the first performer to be a teammate of both Stan Musial and Ken Boyer at the same time that he served as their manager? Be careful; your instinctive guess may lead you astray, so we'll ante a double, plus a RBI for the year he did it.

2 A three-run homer if you know the only skipper to mentor future Cubs pennant-winning manager Charlie Grimm in his rookie season as a Card in 1918 and who later in his managerial career made out a daily lineup card for a full season in Cincinnati that usually included future Dodgers flag-winning pilot Charlie Dressen.

3 He was the first manager who was not at the time also an active player to win a flag at the helm of a St. Louis major league team. The club was the Cards and our man wore a Birds suit during his long baseball career only to sit in their dugout. Triple for him, plus a RBI for the year.

4 Five men who managed the Cardinals also piloted the Browns. All of them did it after 1901, and knowing each member of this quintet will earn you a three-run homer. Snag a triple for four, single for three, zip for anything less.

5 The last ML pitcher to win 20 games in a season in which he also served as a player-manager shepherded the Cards to fifth place before exiting early the following campaign. Learning that he's a Hall of Famer and that fellow Cooperstown inductee Jake Beckley led the club in ribbies that year should direct you to a double for him and two RBI for his 20-win season at the Cards helm.

6 Who steered the first NL team representing St. Louis to win 100 games? RBI double.

7 A decade after this journeyman first sacker closed his 17-year career with the Cards, he assumed the Birds' managerial duties for the final 96 games of the regular season. The Redbirds' last skipper before Tony La Russa, he's good for two.

8 Who was the most recent former big league pitcher to guide the Cards? Before coming to St. Louis, he had served as the most recent pitching player-manager in the majors. Double.

9 Can you name the only Cards player-manager to direct the club for as many as three full seasons and bat .300 or better in each of his campaigns at the Birds wheel? He logged a .543 winning percentage in his first year as the Cards pilot and just a .314 mark with a cellar dweller in his finale. Triple.

10 He won 92 games in his lone season at the Cards helm after winning a MVP Award the previous year. RBI double.

11 In keeping with the Cards' long tradition of drawing from former players within their own flock, prior to Tony La Russa only two skippers since 1900 had guided the Birds for four or more full seasons without ever wearing Cards togs as a player. One, Branch Rickey, had nonetheless played in a Mound City uniform for the Browns. The second man had never previously worn a St. Louis suit in any capacity before piloting the Birds. Name him for a single.

12 A Cards coach for years, he served as interim skipper after the exits of both Frankie Frisch and Ray Blades. It was he who was coaching at third when Enos Slaughter sprinted home with what proved to be the winning run of the 1946 Series. Triple.

13 During his four years of stewardship, this Cards player-manager finished above .500 just once and then by a mere single game. Although many consider him the finest performer at his position during the Deadball Era, his managerial legacy lagged far behind his fiery playing portfolio. Double.

14 Here's your grand slam in this department. Who is the lone man to skipper St. Louis teams in two different major leagues while an active player but never play for the AL Browns, the AA Browns, or the present St. Louis NL franchise? Those who know the history of all the St. Louis ML teams will nail the man who led the majors in batting one memorable season.

AB: 14
Hits: 14
Total Bases: 36
RBI: 16

INNING 8
RED-HOT ROOKIES

1 To date, only one Redbirds rookie in franchise history has won 20 or more games, led the club in winning percentage, and seen Series action, all in his frosh season. Name him for a RBI double, plus another RBI for his sterling rookie campaign.

2 In his yearling season he led the NL in fewest baserunners allowed per nine innings while setting the Cards franchise record for the highest winning percentage by a frosh. Never again an ERA qualifier in his 10-year career, he finished with the 1953 Indians. Double, plus a RBI for his great frosh season.

3 To date, who is the only player to win Rookie of the Year honors on a Cards flag winner? He scored 107 runs and topped the majors in another offensive category in which he set an all-time freshman standard. Routine single, plus a benevolent RBI for nailing his record-setting feat.

4 A couple of earlier bitter cups of coffee with Washington brought him to the Cards in the spring of 1915 at age 25 still in search of a home in the show. He responded with 25 triples to set a new club frosh record that has never been remotely threatened since. Nevertheless, the final result was not a lengthy stay up top—he was gone just two years later. Three-bagger.

5 His frosh year produced 19 homers to set a new Cardinals yearling record (since broken). But his 1.021 OPS in his second campaign still ranks as the highest ever by a Cards soph (minimum 500 PA). RBI double, plus an extra base for our man's first two seasons.

6 Named the starting third baseman for the NL squad in the All-Star Game his rookie year, he was felled by an injury shortly thereafter and held to just 92 games as a yearling. Our palindromic rook left the majors in 1952 having played in just 218 games, all but the last 13 with the Cards. Whose career are we describing for a three-bagger?

7 The same year the above Card exited the majors, a new Redbirds rookie appeared on the horizon and cometed to a 12–2 record with a dazzling 2.72 ERA in 52 hill appearances. But as fast as he rose to prominence he faded into oblivion, falling prey to arm trouble after pitching just one more inning in the majors following his sensational rookie year. Whose career are we describing for another three-bagger?

8 He lasted just one year in Busch country, but that season he paced all NL rooks with just eight homers and 42 ribbies in 97 games while hitting .271. That winter he became the lynchpin in the Bruce Sutter deal but returned to Busch nine years later for his coda season. RBI single, plus an extra ribby for his freshman campaign.

9 In 1930, his official rookie season, he backed up Jimmie Wilson and stung the ball for a cool .366 BA in 76 games. Two years later he claimed the Cards' first-string catching job but held it for only one year before he was traded to the Giants. He later returned to the Cards and served as their regular receiver in 1941. Though he never matched his red-hot rookie year, he played 17 seasons in the NL, finishing with the 1945 Phils. Two-run double.

10 After trying him briefly over three seasons, the Cards gave him his first real shot in 1938, as he made 25 starts and relieved in 22 others to lead ML rooks with 47 appearances. He also paced NL frosh in innings and strikeouts while topping Redbirds qualifiers in ERA. A toughie even for Birds die-hards, so we'll award a bases-clearing triple for this righty who died in St. Louis in 1987.

11 What Cards backup gardener was never able to win a regular job in the bigs despite slamming .374 in 92 games and posting a 1.019 OPS in his official rookie year for the only Birds club that lost a World Series to the Philadelphia A's? Three-bagger for him, plus a RBI for the year.

12 His 18 wins topped all NL rookies in 1945, and he followed with six victories in spot duty for the pitching-rich Cards flag winner the following year. The bottom fell out on his hill career in 1947, but he later enjoyed a lengthy stay as a NL umpire. Three bases.

13 Second sacker Miller Huggins joined the Cards in 1910. All of 5'6½", he was paired with a 5'6" rookie shortstop who remained his keystone companion for three full seasons. Nail that 1910 frosh shortstop who was called "Pee Wee" for a two-run homer.

14 Currently the 25 most prolific winners in Cards franchise history range from Bob Gibson with 251 victories to Red Munger with 74. All but one of the 25 list members spent his rookie year with the Cards. Who is the only hurler on the list whose official frosh season was served in the threads of another ML team? We'll note that he won more games as a Bird than either Steve Carlton or Murry Dickson and had previously chalked up exactly 100 victories with his original team before the Cards acquired him in a memorable trade. Two-run double.

AB: 14
Hits: 14
Total Bases: 35
RBI: 16

INNING 9
FALL CLASSICS

1 What gardener began a season with a Cards club that would advance to the Series but wound up competing against the Redbirds in that year's Fall Classic? His new team beat the Birds in seven games, as he batted .333 just three years after he poked .321 in fall action for a Cards world champ. A regular for both clubs, he's good for two, plus a RBI for his victorious AL club and the year he played with both Series participants.

2 In their 1931 fall triumph over the A's, the Cards employed three different third basemen. All three started at least one game and each served as the club's leadoff hitter in at least one game. Owing to a nagging knee injury, the man who'd been the Birds' regular third sacker for most of the season started just one of the seven contests. Name him and either of his two third-cushion alternates for a three-bagger. Two RBI if you know both alternates.

3 When this Card took the hill one October, he set a new record for the fewest regular season wins (5) by any opening Series contest starter in history. He's good for one base. But you can stretch it to a double by naming the opposing tosser this Redbird defeated in the first Fall Classic lid-lifter that featured two frosh starters.

4 The Cards employed four second-line pitchers as relievers in the 1926 World Series. Which of the following members of the Cards staffs in the late 1920s was not one of the four? Vic Keen, Art Reinhart, Bill Hallahan, Hi Bell, Clarence Mitchell. Two-bagger.

5 Jeff Lahti was the Cards' primary regular-season stopper, but this lefty earned both of the Birds' saves during the 1985 NLCS, including the clincher, and then bagged a victory in Game 2 of the World Series. Do you recall him for a double?

6 Four men tied for the hit lead in the 1934 Series with 11 apiece. One was Detroit second sacker Charlie Gehringer; the other three were all Cardinals. Name the trio for a three-bagger. One base if you know only two. Zilch for just one.

7 On October 11, 1964, the Cards beat the Yanks 4–3 in Game 4 of the World Series with all the Birds' runs coming on one swing from this man. He remains the only bammer to account for all his team's runs in a Series win via a grand-slam homer. Sure-bet single.

8 The hero of the Cards' surprise 1942 fall triumph over the Yankees was a rookie hurler who tossed two complete-game wins. Name him for a deuce.

9 Two Birds twirlers have logged complete-game shutout wins over the Yankees in fall action. One did it in the Cards' first Series home game as a member of the NL, and the other was a lefty who got the job done in Yankee Stadium in the only postseason box score in which he ever appeared. The first is a Hall of Famer and worth only a RBI single, but knowing the southpaw on the 1942 squad as well will bring the answer up to a two-run triple.

10 Between 1985 and 1987, this Cards backup infielder collected 122 at bats without hitting a single homer. Yet in the 1987 Series he made his only hit count when he stroked a three-run shot against Frank Viola in Game 4 to give the Birds the lead. It would be a crime if any Redbirds rooters were to forget him for a RBI double.

11 Harry Brecheen, the 1946 fall hero, was neither the first nor the most recent pitcher to win three games in a World Series, but prior to Randy Johnson in 2001, he was the only twirler to collect his three victories without performing a certain task that every other Series three-game winner performed. For a double, what was it?

12 We're anteing a double that you've forgotten the Card who led all regulars on both sides in batting when he slapped .412 during the 1987 classic.

13 In the 1942 World Series, the St. Louis native who played a majority of the games at second base for the Cards in the regular season was restricted to one appearance as a pinch runner. Nail this eerie World War II casualty for a two-bagger, plus two RBI for the infielder who replaced him at second and led all Cards Series regulars with a .300 BA.

14 Score a RBI single for naming the only hurler to toil for the Cards in both the 2004 and 2006 Series?

15 The name of the only Cardinals position player to see action in every Series game in the Birds' first four fall appearances—1926, 1928, 1930, and 1931—is worth another RBI single. The one clue you should need is that a sub gardener prevented a second performer from making the same claim. Extra RBI for the second man who missed sharing the distinction when he was subbed for in one game.

AB: 15
Hits: 15
Total Bases: 30
RBI: 11

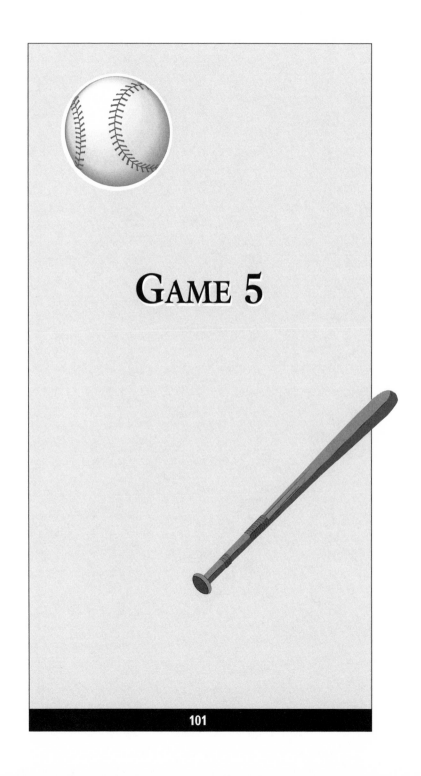

GAME 5

INNING 1
ALL IN THE FAMILY

Perhaps the most famous pair of relatives in Cardinals franchise history is the Dean brothers, but there are other Birds of a feather that are just as significant in their own right.

1 No ML club has featured three brothers on the same team in one season since the Cards sported this sibling trio. The eldest and most talented of the troika retired with over 2,200 career hits and fathered a lad who blasted over 30 homers in back-to-back seasons in the junior loop. RBI double for knowing all three bros, an extra base for the year, plus a bonus ribby for pegging the star's son.

2 What Cards duo featured the only pitching brother teammates in ML history to date to appear in the same postseason game? Sharing that they won 31 games combined that season will steer you off the Deans and, we hope, to their doorstep for a single, plus a RBI for the year.

3 He saw postseason mound action with the Cards in three separate seasons and logged a 101–69 career mark in Birds threads. His son experienced postseason fare as both an infielder and a pilot and outhit his pitching father by only 43 points in the course of a 10-year playing career. Double for this lefty and his light-hitting offspring.

4 We're feeling charitable, so pocket a single by naming the Cards freshman who parked 22 homers one year in just 280 at bats while his dad looked on in the Redbirds dugout.

5 As a Card, he lost a postseason contest ignominiously in a 14–0 drubbing 32 years after his father dropped a deciding World Series game against the Redbirds. Restore the family's pride and name them both for a single, plus a RBI if you know the years they tasted October defeat.

6 His son played for the other city in Missouri and, at that, for only 20 games in 1969. Dad played against the first Kansas City AL entry in the latter part of the 1950s after a long NL career that included three seasons with the Cards. Pop's best Redbirds numbers came in 1948 when he hammered senior-loop pitchers for a .321 BA and a .528 SA in 96 games. RBI triple.

7 His first ML appearance was with the 1953 Cards as an 18-year-old Bonus Baby. His only Series cut in a Birds uniform came 15 years later in his second stint in St. Loo. His son earned post-season moolah with the 1986 Angels and finished his career 10 years later where it began—in Anaheim. Two-run double.

8 The first two brothers in ML history to play beside one another in the same infield occupied short and third for the Cards' oldest ancestor—the 1882 St. Louis Browns. Both were lifelong St. Louis residents and served as Mound City firemen after their playing careers ended. Two-run triple.

9 In five seasons with the Birds, this righty appeared in over 140 games as a starter-reliever before traveling to seven other teams and retiring with over 1,500 innings and a woeful 4.67 ERA. His papa, a pastureman, teamed with Stan Musial for 24 games over a two-year spread in the early 1960s before exiting the show. The last name of these players with Puerto Rican roots is worth one base, but advance to second for adding their first names too.

10 The second sibling pair to don Cards red and white as teammates in postseason play were feature performers on three straight St. Louis NL champs. You should need to know no more than that in his ML debut the younger sib caught his brother. RBI single.

11 Don't expect more than a single for naming the lone father and son with World Series rings earned for their on-the-field con-tributions to the Cards. However, we'll add a generous RBI if you peg both of their World Championship seasons.

12 The lone member of the five Delahanty brothers to perform for a St. Louis NL entry was a regular on both the 1908 and 1909 crews. A Card for his entire ML career, he finished with a .238 career BA, a mere 108 points below that of his most famous sibling, Ed. Three-bagger.

13 Sonny boy captured AL Rookie of the Year honors, slugging 22 homers 22 years after dad played over 100 games with one of Schoendienst's crews. Single for the kid, but add an extra base for knowing his proud pop.

14 His brother never wore Redbirds flannels but did see brief duty as a Washington gardener in two separate ML stints eight years apart. He, on the other hand, was a continuous diamond presence in St. Louis for 14 straight years—12 with the Cards and two with the Browns. Learning that he was almost universally acclaimed to have been the Cards' best performer at his position during the club's first century of existence merits you only a single.

> **AB:** 14
> **Hits:** 14
> **Total Bases:** 26
> **RBI:** 11

INNING 2
RBI RULERS

1 In 1923, Rogers Hornsby racked up a .627 slugging average but collected just 83 RBI. What fellow infielder and future Brooklyn third-base coach unexpectedly led the Cards that year with 96 RBI despite tagging just two home runs and posting a weak .697 OPS? Two-run homer.

2 The season record holder for the most RBI by a performer who etched 20 or more doubles, triples, and home runs each that same year is a Cardinal. His 136 ribbies were accompanied by 42 doubles, 31 homers, and 20 three-baggers. He's worth a RBI single, and his big year rates an extra base.

3 What Cardinal once knocked home 101 runs despite amassing just 17 doubles and 11 home runs? We'll add that his 12 triples that year are the most since 1900 by a Cards player older than age 35 and grant a two-bagger for him plus a RBI for his last 100-ribby season.

4 What Card qualified for the batting title one year and hit over .330 with a .953 OPS, 17 homers, and 54 extra base hits, yet managed to drive in just 62 runs? Was his problem that he hit low in the order? Not hardly. The clue that it was his career low in RBI for a season in which he qualified for the bat title shaves this to a RBI double, plus a second ribby for his "off" year.

5 Would you believe that in 1925 a Card eclipsed the above man when he amassed 57 extra base hits, a .958 OPS, and 112 runs while totaling just 57 RBI. A Bird for his entire 10-year career, he finished in 1932 with a .301 career BA after returning to the club in 1930 following a trip back to the minors the previous year. Two-run homer.

6 Who are the only two Cards to register 100 extra base hits and 100 RBI in the same season? Need both names for a single, plus an extra base if you also know each of their super seasons.

7 During his first season in Redbirds garb he plated a club-leading 105 runs for Hutch's crew after posting six 100-ribby seasons with his previous NL outfit. Thereafter, his career swiftly nosedived, and two years later he was through at age 34. A vastly underrated run producer of his era, he rates a RBI single.

8 Who was the youngest Card to plate 100+ mates in a season? He eclipsed Joe Medwick's long-standing youngest mark and bettered Medwick's total by 24 ribbies. Single, plus a RBI for the year.

9 This lefty swinger never drove home more than 76 runs during his lengthy career and stands as the Cards record holder for most career RBI without ever totaling 100 in a season. Single.

10 The most recent NLer to fan 25 times or less during a 100 RBI season is this performer who played in five World Series and made Cooperstown. Double, plus a RBI for the year he sported exemplary bat control.

11 As of 2008, two players have led the Cards in RBI for seven straight seasons. One should be a cinch, but the other might surprise you. Triple for both, just a single for knowing one.

12 Who led the last Cards flag winner managed by Red Schoendienst in RBI? Just 79 ribbies was all he needed to take top honors after driving in 77 the year before when he fell 34 behind Cepeda. Let's go for two here.

13 What Hall of Famer drove in over 100 runs three straight years with the Birds, two of them for flag winners, but led the club in RBI just once when he posted 95 for yet a third Cards flag winner? Single, plus a RBI for his three-year 100-ribby skein.

14 Who led the Cards in cumulative RBI during the decade of the 1960s (1961–1970)? Despite his accomplishments as a Redbird, we're wagering a double that you'll guess wrong here.

AB: 14
Hits: 14
Total Bases: 29
RBI: 12

1 Since the Cy Young's inception in 1956, no Card has won more games in a season without winning the award than this 27-year-old righty, who finished third in that year's balloting. Single, plus a RBI for the year.

2 A 21-game loser generally doesn't draw much Cy Young interest, but a 21-game loser for a certain Mound City entry would have been a near unanimous selection. The only hurler in franchise history to lose more than nine games in a season in which he logged a sub-2.00 ERA balanced that by leading his loop in both wins and ERA and in so doing spurred his club to its fourth straight pennant. Try for two bases here, plus an extra base for his regal year.

3 What Redbird was the first man to notch a Cy Young vote while working almost exclusively from the pen? Your clue that he teamed with Stan the Man that year reduces this to a RBI single.

4 Who led the Cards in almost every major pitching department in the Birds' only World Series year in which they wore both their home and road uniforms for games played in their home park? Single for the chucker, plus a gift RBI for the year.

5 Dizzy Dean and this Cy Young honoree are the only Cards hillmen to record winning percentages of .800+ during a season when they won at least 20 games. Single, plus a RBI for this other ace's award-winning year.

6 For a single, name the Cards hurler who died just two seasons after notching eight Cy Young votes during a 20-win campaign.

7 No Cards chucker has ever won a Cy Young after beginning the season with another team, but a certain Redbirds twirler likely would have perpetrated this feat had the award existed the year he paced the NL with 23 wins. The final 21 came as a Bird after an early-season deal sprang him loose from the Boston Braves, for whom he had gone 9–16 the previous year. Three-bagger for the hurler and an extra base for his big season with the Cards.

8 Currently just one Cards hillman born outside the U.S. has ever earned Cy Young votes, and he did it three times, placing fourth in consecutive seasons in Birds threads. Single for him, plus an extra base for his homeland.

9 He led the only World Series entrant that featured Joe Garagiola with 21 wins to make a strong case for retroactive Cy Young honors. Take a RBI single, but only if you know both the pitcher and the year.

10 Standing 6'6", this broad-shouldered righty won a career-high 18 games after signing as a free agent but received no decisions in three starts during that postseason. Nine baseball writers gave him Cy Young votes for his efforts, and you can earn a single for his name and a RBI for the year.

11 In 1914 the Cardinals saw third-place heights for the first time since they'd joined the NL. What hurler stood to vie for loop pitching honors that year after sparking the Birds with a 19–6 record and a loop-leading 1.72 ERA? RBI double.

12 Great things were expected from this 6'6" Cards lefty, and it looked like he might deliver on the hype after earning seven Cy Young votes as an 18-game winner in Redbirds flannels. But, alas, an elbow injury ruined his promising career. Later a color commentator for the Devil Rays, this Iowa-born flameout will get you to first.

13 Prior to Bob Gibson in 1968, who was the last Cardinal to win 20 games and lead the NL in ERA in the same season? It was his career year, as he also led the NL in strikeouts, shutouts, and winning percentage. Worth only a single, with a RBI for his Cy Young–worthy campaign.

14 It's no secret that Bob Gibson logged the lowest ERA to date (1.12) for a Cy Young–winning starter. But what Birds moundsman posted the highest ERA in history among all NL Cy Young winners to date? Double.

> **AB:** 14
> **Hits:** 14
> **Total Bases:** 22
> **RBI:** 9

INNING 4
ODD COMBO
ACHIEVEMENTS

Babe Ruth held the ML records for both the most career home runs and the most career batters strikeouts when he retired. In this section, you'll meet former Cardinals who also hold odd and often contradictory club and ML records.

1 The pitcher who holds the Cards' all-time season record among ERA qualifiers for the fewest hits yielded per nine innings ironically also owns the club standard for most career wild pitches. Charity starts here with a single.

2 It was this early-day Card's all-time record that Lou Brock broke when he swiped his 370th base as a Bird. But nobody will ever touch our man's franchise record for the most career errors (462) in Mound City garb. Nail this master at both pilfering and giving up a free base and score a two-run double.

3 In his rookie year he was the only Cards pitcher to break .500 and thus led the club in winning percentage. Two years later he again led the club in winning percentage with a stellar .625 mark. Nevertheless, in his four and a half seasons as a Card, he posted the lowest career winning percentage (.437) of any hurler who tossed a minimum of 1,000 innings with the club since 1901. Learning that his real first name was Henry and that he co-led the NL in wins in 1926 should make you pause to wipe your goggles and then streak to a two-run double.

4 The player who holds the officially documented record for the most times caught stealing by a rookie also claims the all-time ML mark for most consecutive thefts without being caught. Single.

5 At the close of World War II, he held the Cards record for the most career home runs by a player at his position, and he still owns the Birds' all-time franchise mark for the most career sacrifice hits with 154. It's no surprise to find him the early home run leader at his position, but you'll surprise us to the tune of a triple if you know that he remains the Birds career sac hit leader.

6 In 1998 a certain Cardinal experienced perfection as a pitcher, hitter, and fielder when he went 4–0, batted 1.000, and also fielded 1.000. A year later he dropped to a .444 winning percentage, hit .000, and fielded a weak .938. Born in England, this ephemerally flawless lefty who ended his career with a .154 BA and a 5.24 ERA is worth a RBI single.

7 He played only five seasons with the Cards but nonetheless is the career franchise leader in being hit by pitches with 87. In addition, he set the present franchise season record with 31 in a year that he batted only .241. The second surprise? He was not a middle infielder. The clue that he led the Federal League in slugging and triples in 1914 should aid you to score a RBI three-bagger here.

8 Since intentional walks officially began being recorded in 1955, he holds the Cards career record at 151. However, he also currently sports the club's season mark for hitting into double plays, with 29. Take two for this slow poke who nonetheless induced opposing hurlers to pitch to him selectively.

9 In his official frosh season, he set the Cards' post-1900 record for wild pitches with 19 while also setting the club's post-1900 rookie record for wins with 23. His name brings a RBI double, plus an extra base for his contradictory frosh season.

10 Among all ML performers in a minimum of 600 games at shortstop, this longtime Mound City denizen's .860 career fielding average is the all-time lowest. He also holds the record for the most games played in a St. Louis ML uniform (659) by a performer who never appeared in either the National or the American League. Enough here to strut to a home run.

11 Not only does he hold the Cards career standard for lowest SA (.344) among Redbirds with at least 5,000 plate appearances, but he also owns the team record for fewest homers (27) with that many trips to the plate. Need we mention that he also owns numerous other club and NL records, most of them positive? Single.

12 At the time of his retirement, he held the Cards' post-1892 (when they entered the NL) record for the fewest career walks (213) among all players who collected a minimum of 3,000 at bats as Redbirds. That mark has since been broken, but he still owns the Cards franchise record for the fewest career strikeouts (105) among all players who batted a minimum of 3,000 times in Birds garb since batter strikeouts began being recorded on an annual basis. Who was this contact hitter extraordinaire who swung from both sides of the plate at almost everything and seldom missed? Sing his song and win a three-run triple.

13 Ten hurlers have heaved as many as 1,500 innings with the Cardinals. The leader among the 10 in fewest walks per nine innings was also the club leader for over 30 years in most strikeouts per nine innings. Name this rare fireballer with outstanding control and bag a RBI single.

14 Set your sights on this Redbird who became the first player in ML history to tag fewer than 200 homers while fanning over 1,500 times. If that wasn't bad enough, he also committed the most career errors (196) of any NL outfielder who debuted since the Deadball Era. How'd this bum hang around so long? Just maybe he set a few positive records in his day as well. Single.

AB: 14
Hits: 14
Total Bases: 28
RBI: 12

INNING 5
MVP MARVELS

1 What Cardinal won the first Baseball Writers' Association of America MVP Award given to a NL player in 1931? RBI single.

2 Among all players who have debuted since the BBWAA's MVP honor was established, who played the most career games in a Cards suit without ever earning a MVP vote? His glove and strong arm kept him anchored in the Birds infield for eight years, the last of which earned him an All-Star berth. Although never a big threat with the stick, he was a notoriously strong April hitter and once clubbed 17 homers in a season. RBI single.

3 The first NL MVP prize was given in 1911 and was called the Chalmers Award. The Cards' highest finisher in the initial balloting came in sixth, just behind a Phils rookie pitcher named Alexander. Later our man became the first switch-hitter to make the Hall of Fame, albeit not entirely for his playing accomplishments. Name him for a two-run double.

4 The Cards' highest finisher in any of the four seasons when the Chalmers Award was given secured fifth place in 1914. It was his first season as a Bird after coming west from Pittsburgh, where he'd been a member of the 1909 World Championship crew. RBI triple.

5 The Cards' first league MVP winner was a member of the 1925 entry. He finished third in the balloting in 1927 but by then was wearing a different NL uniform. Single for him, extra base for his 1927 team.

6 The first right-handed pitcher to win a BBWAA award toiled for a Mound City NL entry. Who was it? RBI double, plus an extra base for his triumphant year.

7 He failed to crack the senior-circuit's top 10 in batting, slugging, or OBP and tied for second in grounding into double plays. Yet he copped the NL MVP handily by more than 50 votes over the runner-up. Clearly his glove work and the Cards' finish that season aided him in the balloting. Single, plus a RBI for the year.

8 Who was the first member of the Cards franchise to win more than one MVP prize? Single for him, plus two RBI for his first and second award years.

9 During his lone season with the Cards, this 6'5" right-hander made the All-Star team and set a ML record (later broken) for saves by a bullpenner (36) in his final ML season while earning the only MVP vote any Redbird notched in that year's balloting. He hailed from Kansas City, Mo., and will bring you a RBI single, plus an extra base for the year.

10 Only one Cardinal earned MVP votes in 1993, and he was the sole Redbird to do so in 1994 as well. Those were his only two seasons in the Mound City, and he made the All-Star team on both occasions. Single.

11 A certain performer won a MVP with the Birds by hitting 66 points higher in his award-winning year than during his 18-year career composite and posting an OPS more than 150 points above his career mark. Single, plus a RBI for the year.

12 The 1946 world champs had three of the top four finishers in the NL MVP race that year. Name them for a double, plus two RBI for knowing the non-Cardinal who finished second that year.

13 Lou Brock never won a MVP during his long career. In fact he cracked the top five in the balloting just once in his 19 seasons, placing second. For a RBI single, what year was it?

14 Joe Medwick was far from a unanimous NL MVP selection in 1937 even though he won the Triple Crown. What other Hall of Famer trailed him by just two votes in the NL MVP balloting that year? Double.

AB: 14
Hits: 14
Total Bases: 23
RBI: 14

INNING 6
HOME RUN KINGS

1 Aptly nicknamed "Home Run," he crushed 16 round-trippers as a St. Louis rookie in 1889 despite hitting just .244. His tater total remained the ML mark until 1914 for the most by a player with a sub-.250 batting average, and it will always be the record for the highest season total by a member of the Cards franchise prior to the establishment of the present pitching distance in 1893. Three-run homer.

2 The most recent Card to slug 30+ home runs and pole as many as 10 triples in the same season played 11 years with the Redbirds and died in the Mound City in 1982. Two-bagger, plus a RBI for the year.

3 He paced a Cards team with 13 homers, matching his total from the previous year on a Redbirds flag winner for which he fell nine shy of the club leader, Jack Clark. It was him the Birds swapped to the Bucs along with two others for Tony Pena. Single.

4 Only three hot-corner denizens to date have tagged as many as 100 career homers in Redbirds bunting. Knowing the first member of the trio to do it will garner a double.

5 When Jack Clark averaged 8.35 home runs for every 100 at bats in 1987, whose old club mark of 7.74 (including batting-title qualifiers only) did he break? Your clue is the former record holder eclipsed his own club mark of 6.74, set three years prior to his 7.74 season. The player's worth only a single, but his two big homer years will bring an extra two bases.

6 Prior to expansion, the Cards record for the fewest walks (30) by a player who hit 20 or more home runs belonged to a Hall of Famer who never walked more than 45 times in a season. Name this free-swinger for a RBI double.

7 Only one bat-title qualifier in Cards history (minimum 400 AB) has registered a .400+ slugging average in a season in which he failed to hit a home run. He struck .314 that year for a flag winner and the following year led the NL in doubles while appearing in his second straight World Series. In a 13-year career, ending with Cincinnati in 1934, he poked just nine taters in 5,557 at bats. Clues are plentiful, but we still think this should generate a triple.

8 Until Albert Pujols happened on the scene, who was the last Cards first sacker to thump 20+ homers in a season? Simple, right? A RBI single says you're wrong.

9 Prior to expansion it was a rare hitter who pasted as many as 20 homers in a season while posting a sub-.750 OPS. In fact, just two Cards held that dubious distinction. Amazingly, both achieved it in the same season. The year was 1953; one performer was a rookie and the other was in his first season as a regular. Paste those clues together for a homer of your own if you know both. Zip for less.

10 You'll stump many Mound City hardball mavens by asking them to name the first switch-hitting Cards outfielder to belt as many as 25 homers in a season. A true journeyman, he suited up with eight different teams in 13 seasons, and was last spotted in 2000 during his second stint with the Tribe. We'll also share that he led the Cards the year he went deep exactly 25 times. Double.

11 The owner of the highest season OPS in Cards history by a bat-title qualifier—a rousing 1.245—achieved his record figure long before the term OPS existed and, not surprisingly, won the NL home run crown that season. He's a single and his record year is another base.

12 In 1903 the Cards hit a club post-1900 season record-low eight home runs. It was also the lowest total that year in the majors. What gardener smote four of the eight dingers to lead the team? Two-run homer in every sense.

13 We don't just ask about the big sticks—especially not when the last hitter prior to Juan Pierre in 2007 to total 700+ PA during a season in which he failed to homer was a Cardinal who turned the trick with a Redbirds Series entrant. Name him for a single, plus a RBI for the year.

14 Five men to date have collected 100 or more home runs, triples, and doubles while serving in Cards livery. Name all five for a double, sac hit for four, zero for less.

15 Who was the only receiver to hit as many as 50 career dingers in Cards red prior to NL expansion in 1962? It was his mark of 60 that Tim McCarver broke. Run hard, don't walk, and you can snare a triple.

AB: 15
Hits: 15
Total Bases: 36
RBI: 10

INNING 7
RED-HOT ROOKIES

1 Prior to 1982, who held the Cards franchise record for both the most home runs by a rookie (21) and the most sacrifice flies in a season with 11? His two club marks were set in back-to-back years. The sac-fly record fell in 1982, but his rookie tater standard was good for nearly two more decades. RBI double.

2 He saw spot work for two Cards flag winners before enjoying his official freshman campaign where he rewarded the Birds at 10–4, good for a .714 winning percentage. Although he failed to garner any Rookie of the Year votes, he retired 15 years later with 185 victories. Single, plus a RBI for his first full season.

3 In the Cards' 1967 pennant season, this righty strutted his stuff from the pen, pacing NL rooks with 65 appearances and tying for the loop's top yearling honors with 10 saves. What's more, he relieved in three Series games that year. Cancer tragically claimed his life at age 34. We'll wager a triple that he's slipped beneath your synapses.

4 The top rookie shortstop in the majors in 1929, he rapped .262 in 146 games for the Cards and remained one of the NL's best middle infielders through the 1932 campaign. A hunting accident that winter sidelined him until 1935 and prevented him from ever again seeing regular duty in the majors. Name him for a triple.

5 After a brief trial the year before, he was employed by the Cards as an outfielder-catcher in 1958 and stroked .281 with 13 homers in 137 games during his lone season as a Redbirds regular. Three years later he led the expansion Senators with 18 clouts in just 364 at bats. He died in St. Louis, where he managed a cocktail lounge, when he was only 47. Solo homer.

6 In 1899, thanks to syndicate ownership, St. Louis fell heir to almost the entire Cleveland Spiders roster of the previous year. But it was clever scouting that brought the Mound City outfit a rookie from the California League whose .323 frosh season, albeit in just 66 games, would be 10 points below his final career average when he left the majors 15 years later. At the time he departed, his .333 figure ranked 10th among all retired players who had appeared in 500 or more ML games. Unhappily for St. Louisans, only his first two ML seasons were spent in Missouri. RBI triple.

7 Following a brief call-up the year before, this Card led senior-loop frosh in games with 152 while playing all three outfield positions and everywhere in the infield. However, Redbirds rooters may remember him best as the performer who set their rookie hitting streak record at 25. Single, plus a RBI for the year.

8 The 1919 season produced no rookies who qualified for the NL batting title. The Cards were the only senior-loop club that even had a freshman who played in over half of his team's games. A catcher no less, he took over the Birds' first-string job by the end of the season and held it for the next two years, reaching his apex in 1921 when he rapped .320 in 117 games. Never more than a sub thereafter, the NL's rookie leader in games, at bats, and hits in 1919 can put a two-run homer in your column.

9 Although this lefty previously appeared with Houston, his official rookie year came while wearing Cards duds. That season he posted a team-topping 13 saves, with a shimmering 1.54 ERA in 57 appearances. In his four-year Redbirds sojourn, he appeared in two World Series, totaling five games. Double, plus a RBI for his sparkling yearling campaign.

10 In his 11-year career he compiled a .390 on base percentage but just a .411 slugging average. Arriving in the show to stay at age 28, he promptly set a new Cards rookie record for walks with 75. Though his active playing career ended nearly half a century ago, his club frosh free-pass record still stands. Who is he? Double.

---

11 Would you believe the 1965 Cards started a certain rookie fledgling three times and he won each contest, all of them complete games? What's so special about that? His trio of route-going efforts led all NL freshmen that year! Later a member of the Birds starting rotation for three years, this southpaw's good for three.

12 In his first full season he paced NL rooks with 12 victories and also surrendered future teammate Lou Brock's first career homer. The dinger clue narrows down the era and adding that this chucker spent all but his 10th and final season in Redbirds threads makes him good for a single, plus a gift RBI for the year.

13 In the Cards franchise's inaugural season of 1882 when the team was known as the Browns and was a member of the American Association, just about every player that made the club's spring cut and opened the AA season was a rookie as per today's frosh rules. Can you identify the only one of the following roster members of the original Cards franchise that had previously played at least one full season in the National League, thereby according him veteran status? Charlie Comiskey, Jumbo McGinnis, Bill Gleason, Oscar Walker, Bill Smiley, Jack Shappert, Harry McCaffery. RBI triple.

14 This swift Cards center fielder led all ML freshmen in runs (81) and steals (30) while stroking 173 hits in 559 at bats for a neat .309 BA. Rewarded at season's end, he became the first Redbirds yearling to capture the NL Rookie of the Year Award in 19 seasons. Single, plus a RBI for the year.

AB: 14
Hits: 14
Total Bases: 33
RBI: 11

INNING 8
THE NAME'S THE SAME

There has been only one performer in Cardinals lore named Musial and only one Hornsby, Medwick, and Schoendienst. But there have been multiple Smiths, Jacksons, and Moores. The questions in this category depict two or more Cardinals players with the same last name. Test yourself on your ability to determine both the last and first names of the players involved in each query.

1 The Cards All-Star who slapped .294 in 1943, the Birds lefty who started the 1935 All-Star Game, and the five-time NL All-Star who closed his career with the Cards in 2005. Double, but you need all three to score.

2 The slugger who led the 1970 Cards in homers and ribbies in his lone year in the Mound City, the starter-reliever who bagged 10 wins with the 1983 Cards after arriving in a June swap, and the 13-year outfielder with a .300 career BA who hit just .241 in 91 games for the 1933 Cards. Triple for all three, single for two.

3 The Cards' 40-year-old reliever who appeared in 42 games in 1974, the reserve second sacker who played over 350 games with the Birds starting in 1990, and the Cards All-Star catcher who posted a ML-leading .997 FA in his final Mound City campaign. Triple for all three, single for two.

4 The Cards' leading run producer in 1914 who divided his time between first base and shortstop, the St. Louis NL entry's leading hitter in 1894 who split his time between third base and catcher, and the owner of a horrendous 5.56 ERA in 1953 who apportioned his time between the pen and starting assignments. Triple for all three, single for only two.

5 The hurler who led the 1902 Cards in wins, the Mound City batsman who led all hitters in the majors in 1887, and the first backstopper in Cards franchise history to catch his brother in a ML game. Two-run double for all three, single for only two.

6 The Redbirds starter who went a deplorable 3–10 in 1992, the eagle-eyed Card who led the NL in walks in 1987, and the six-time All-Star who closed his career smashing .345 in 171 at bats with the 2000 Cards. Double, but you need all three to score.

7 The Cards' leading winner in 1958, the Redbird who tied for the club lead in losses in 1900, and the Cards' regular first baseman in 1948 and most of 1949. Two-run homer for all three, double for two.

8 The Cards outfielder in the early 1920s who sired a son who was the only manager the Seattle Pilots ever had, the Cards rookie reliever in 1955 who later saved 14 games for a Redbirds World Series winner after disappearing from the show for the better part of five years following his frosh season, and the Cards middle reliever who logged a sterling 6–1 record to go with a 2.32 ERA in 40 appearances in 1977. Homer for all three, two bases for two.

9 The only Cards third sacker to lead the NL in doubles, the only Redbirds performer to bat under .200 the season following a 100 RBI campaign with the Birds, and the only pitcher to debut with the Cards and notch all of his 194 career victories with the Pirates. Home run for all three, single for only two.

10 The shortstop that St. Louis owner Chris Von der Ahe labeled the goat for his erratic fielding in the Browns' 1888 World Series loss to the New York Giants and a later-day first baseman on a Cardinals World Champion share the same first and last names. Knock a three-bagger.

11 The Cards rookie right fielder in 1904 who slapped .280 and led all NL gardeners in fielding average, the one-time heir apparent to the Cards shortstop post who played all of 65 games in the majors with the 1959–1960 Birds editions, and the third sacker who spent his entire 882-game career with the Cards and was a member of three Redbirds flag winners. Grand slam for all three, double if you know only two.

12 The Cards' regular third sacker in 1951 who led the NL in fielding average after arriving in May of that season from the junior loop, the 17-year vet who won 12 games during his only full season with the Birds in 1937, and the reserve outfielder who hit just .223 in 81 games for the 1967 Cards World Champions but later won an AL bat crown. RBI triple for all three, single for two.

13 The 1964 Card who tied for the NL lead in relief wins, the Redbirds' club save leader in 1970, and the latter man's teammate who poked .249 in over 100 games that same season. Triple for the trio, single for two.

14 The Cards rookie who went 8–11 in 1905 and finished his ML career in 1913 with an abysmal 51–103 log, the infielder who led the NL in at bats and the Birds in fewest strikeouts per at bat in 1939, and the owner of 657 career stolen bases and nearly 2,000 hits who was expected to fill the club's centerfield hole in 1895 but was packed off to Washington when he hit all of .220 in his 84-game sojourn in St. Louis. RBI triple for all three, single for two.

15 The catcher who stroked .325 on the 1929 Cards, the Birds' regular right fielder in 1914 who led the NL in fielding average, and a Card who played in every game of the 2006 World Series. Triple for all three, single for two.

AB: 15
Hits: 15
Total Bases: 46
RBI: 12

INNING 9
MASTER MOUNDSMEN

1 A round-tripper is yours for the name of the first hurler to win 100 games for a ML team nicknamed the Cardinals. He's also the lone slab man to date to win that many for the Cards and log a sub-.500 record with the club. The clues are thin here, which is why the score is so high.

2 Which of these longtime Mound City mound mainstays won the most games in his tenure with the Cards? Red Munger, Max Lanier, Howie Pollet, Gerry Staley, Bill Hallahan. RBI single.

3 Four slab men posted sub-3.00 ERAs while working a minimum of 1,000 innings in Cardinals raiment between the close of the Deadball Era and NL expansion in 1962. Only one of the four is in the Hall of Fame, and his 2.99 career ERA as a Card is the highest of the quartet. Name all four for a homer. Single if you get as many as three.

4 When Bob Gibson notched his 31st shutout en route to his present Cards club record of 56, whose old team mark of 30 did he break? Two-run double.

5 He pitched on three Cards flag winners during his seven-year tour with the club. Serving as both a starter and a reliever, he won in double figures three times for the Cards, including 1929, when he led the team in winning percentage, shutouts, and ERA. All told, he spent 19 years in the majors, beginning with the 1922 Tigers and finishing with the 1940 Phils. Even with all that info, we think you're still a longshot to unload a two-run jack here.

6 Who was the first lefty in the expansion era to win 20 games for a Cards team that failed to win the pennant? It shouldn't take you long to single here, but snag an extra base for the year.

7 The Cards suffered a long drought after they first joined the NL in 1892 but since then have been the NL's strongest team. Consequently only five Redbirds who have logged as many as 100 decisions with the club own losing career records as Cardinals. Which of these tossers is not among the five? Lee Meadows, Bob Harmon, Vinegar Bend Mizell, Bill Sherdel. Single.

8 Who presently stands to be the last Cards hurler to lose 20 games in a season? We're bound to say it's been a while, and he is also currently one of the two most recent Cards pitchers to lose as many as 19 games in a season. Double for the hurler, two RBI for the year he dropped 20 on the nose.

9 His 45 wins are a Cards franchise season record and were accompanied by a loop-leading 1.63 ERA and a trip to the World Series. Obviously this happened a good while ago, but if you know exactly when and also our titan's name, you score a deuce.

10 Between 1965 and 1975, Bob Gibson started on Opening Day for the Cards in every season except one. The other mounds-man Red Schoendienst employed bagged only one victory with the Redbirds that year before being sold to the dreaded Cubs. If you think this was some obscure figure who lucked into an Opening Day start, it might interest you to learn that this performer lasted four years longer in the bigs than Gibby. RBI single, plus an extra base for the year he started the Birds' season lid-lifter.

11 Surprise us by naming the only Redbird to date to start at least 30 games for six straight seasons. During his run this tosser led the team in wins just twice, averaged fewer than 13 victories per year, and never completed more than eight starting assignments. Double, plus a RBI for his six-year skein.

12 The Cards have had several fine lefties grace their mound, but the 1990s was not the team's most fertile decade for south-paw talent. What former Birds first-round draft pick notched the club's highest season win total during that period among port-siders with fewer than 15 victories? Serious shoulder injuries destroyed his once promising career. Single.

13 He bagged 16 wins in each of his two seasons with the Cards, leading them in victories once. Far better known for the trade that brought him to St. Louis than for anything he achieved with the club, his name's worth a RBI single.

14 What Cardinal remains the most recent twirler to spin 10 shutouts in a season? Although he failed to earn a single victory in April that year, he won 20 of his last 21 decisions, half of them by a whitewashing. Single, plus a RBI for his superb season.

AB: 14
Hits: 14
Total Bases: 29
RBI: 13

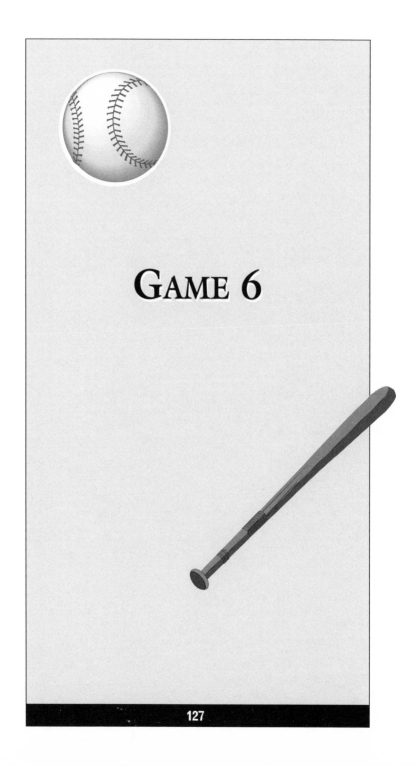

GAME 6

INNING 1
BRAZEN BASE THIEVES

1 Between the Gas House Gang's triumph in 1934 and 1962, the first year of NL expansion, who swiped the most career bases in Cards array? Our announcement that his total, in keeping with an era when thefts were at low ebb, was a rather lackluster 82 reduces this to a RBI double.

2 Prior to 1969, he held the Cards season record for the most at bats (590) without a steal. He's a Hall of Famer but not for his wheels, owning only 42 career thefts as opposed to 2,471 hits. RBI double, plus a second RBI for his record year.

3 In 1891, shortstop Shorty Fuller set a Cards negative franchise record when he swiped 42 bases while hitting just .212. Who is the Birds season leader in thefts since 1900 by a player with a sub-.225 BA? Your clue: a .223 BA accompanied his 30 steals in 1919, but the following year he copped 14 bases while hitting a career high .332. Home run.

4 Which of the following Hall of Famers stole the fewest career bases as a Cardinal? Chick Hafey, Stan Musial, Miller Huggins, Enos Slaughter, Jim Bottomley, Rogers Hornsby. RBI single.

5 Seven pitchers to date have stolen 10 or more career bases while wearing Cards franchise threads. All but one was active primarily in the nineteenth century. Who is the only post-1900 twirler on the list? Two-run triple.

6 Who was the only Redbird between 1928 and 1981 other than Lou Brock to purloin as many as 35 sacks in a season? He led the club that season with 37 swipes, despite posting the lowest OBA (.301) among NL gardeners with at least 500 plate appearances. Birds fans fondly remember him as the man Herzog wisely dumped on Houston straight up for Joaquin Andujar. Double.

7 Although Cardinals speedsters ran wild during the 1980s, only one Redbird filched as many as 40 bases twice during the 1990s. Who was it? Single.

8 Who stole the most career bases in a Cards uniform without ever leading the NL in thefts? In each of his first 12 seasons in the Mound City he pilfered at least 20 sacks, with a high of 57. Single.

9 Since 1900, his 173 thefts are the most in Birds wear among players who swung exclusively from the right side. He stole 68 in his first year at Busch but played just three full seasons in the Mound City before moving on during the following campaign. RBI Single.

10 Which of these speedsters is the only one who was *not* caught stealing at least 100 times in a Cards uniform? Vince Coleman, Ray Lankford, Ozzie Smith, Willie McGee, Lou Brock. Single.

11 What Redbird holds the officially documented NL season mark for most times caught stealing in a season? He's in the Hall of Fame but don't say Brock, because our man died before Lou was even born. Double.

12 Who holds the Cards' post-1900 season mark for steals by a first baseman? In his first year in a Birds suit he filched 46 and then dropped to 12 the next season before moving to the Phils. Hard double, plus a RBI for the year he stacked up the sacks.

13 Arlie Latham swiped 369 bases while in St. Louis garb. No other performer in Cards franchise history has stolen as many as 100 while doing duty at third base. A two-run homer says that you can't name the holder of the Redbirds' post-1900 career record prior to the introduction of division play in 1969 for the most thefts by a hot-corner operative.

14 He set the Birds' post-1900 season record for steals by a second sacker with 55, just one fewer than his personal best established earlier that decade with a club that no longer plays in that city. Double for him, a RBI for his big year in the Mound City, plus an extra base for deducing the other team in question.

15 The Cards have never had a performer rack up 30 homers and 30 steals in the same season, let alone a 40/40 man. Who among the Cards' 40-homer sluggers came the closest to a 40/40 season when he swiped 17 sacks to go with his 42 jacks? He's worth one base; his big year rates a RBI.

> **AB:** 15
> **Hits:** 15
> **Total Bases:** 30
> **RBI:** 13

INNING 2
STELLAR STICKWIELDERS

1 Who rapped over 200 hits despite batting below .300 on a Cards world champ? That year he also smote a personal best 21 homers and 76 RBI, while setting the club season mark with 689 at bats. Cinch single, plus a RBI for the year.

2 Between Stan Musial in 1952 and Albert Pujols in 2003, only one other Cardinal led the NL in total bases. For a RBI single, who was this swatter?

3 This Redbird saw NL pitchers shave nearly 100 points off his average the year after he captured the batting crown, and in so doing they caused him to set the current senior-loop mark for the biggest drop by a reigning hitting titlist in his following season. Single.

4 Who holds the Cards season record for most times reached base? That year he also set the ML record in this category among players who hit below .300. Single, plus a RBI for the year.

5 When a certain Cards chucker rapped 27 hits, he posted the highest total in the majors by a twirler in over 20 years. What's more, this lefty swinger stroked 21 hits the year before, making him the first Redbirds hillman in 35 years to smack at least 20 safeties in consecutive seasons. Single, plus a RBI for his two-year skein.

6 Acquired by the Birds late one year for their pennant drive, this seemingly over-the-hill star astounded everyone, even the Cards, by hitting .434, the highest season BA ever by a Redbird with at least 50 at bats, and, in addition, scalded opposing hurlers for a sizzling 1.213 OPS. In the postseason the magic vanished, as he hit just .167 in the NLCS and only .133 in the Series before leaving the Mound City. A first sacker by then, he served his prime years in center field with another NL outfit. RBI single, plus an extra base for the year.

7 After rapping .304 in over 400 at bats and winning the NL Comeback Player of the Year Award, a certain longtime Cards star opted to quit and never played another big league game. Too much more and we couldn't even award you a single, but add a RBI for the year he bowed out.

8 Nineteen performers between 1882 and NL expansion in 1962 posted career BAs of .300 or better with a minimum of 2,000 plate appearances as members of the Cards franchise. Which of the following list members had the highest career BA to show for his Cards stay? Patsy Donovan, Tommy McCarthy, George Watkins, Joe Cunningham, Frankie Frisch, Ripper Collins, Austin McHenry. Two bases.

9 Following a season as a Cards regular in which he struck just .255, this lefty swinger hiked his average almost 90 points and copped a batting title while slapping 210 hits. Single, plus a RBI for the year.

10 What Cardinal holds the ML season record for singles by a right-handed batter? He's also the only Redbird to top the NL in this category three times, and he did it twice with flag winners. You'll be treading water if you don't nail him for a double.

11 You'd win many a bet if you asked who posted the highest season BA among Cards qualifiers during the 1990s (1991–2000).

It came in his initial year as a Redbird, and he was shifted that season to first base after serving regularly at second and third with his previous outfits. We'll confidently wager two here.

12 His .258 career BA as a Card is the lowest of any player who drilled 1,000+ hits in Birds threads. In addition he posted the worst OPS (.652) of any Redbird who meets the above criteria. Still, he made two All-Star squads and played on three Cardinals flag winners. RBI single.

13 Prior to Albert Pujols, who was the most recent Card to string at least three straight years of 100 RBI while batting .300? Even after we share that the last of those seasons occurred with a Birds flag bearer, this still rates a two-run double.

14 Among stickmen who totaled at least 3,000 PA as Redbirds, which of these performers is the only one with a career BA below .300 in Cards garb? Joe Torre, Garry Templeton, Keith Hernandez, Ripper Collins, Milt Stock, Taylor Douthit. RBI single.

15 Just one Cards regular hit .300 during Whitey Herzog's last full season as Redbirds skipper. That year this swinger also became the first starting NL DH in All-Star history. It was his first full campaign in a Birds suit after leaving another NL club for which he had belted .300+ four times as a bat-title qualifier. RBI single, plus an extra ribby for the year.

AB: 15
Hits: 15
Total Bases: 20
RBI: 13

INNING 3
MEMORABLE MONIKERS

Do you know the full names that go with these nicknames?

1 Blix. RBI triple.

2 Yank. Triple.

3 The Lip. Single.

4 Tacky Tom. Homer.

5 Jumbo (third baseman). Three-run homer.

6 Little Mac. Single.

7 Icebox. Three-run double.

8 Ach. RBI double.

9 Pickles. Double.

10 Parisian Bob. RBI double.

11 Kiko. Single.

12 Chappie. Two-run homer.

13 Skates. Single.

14 Pancho. Triple.

15 The Cat. Two-run single.

> **AB:** 15
> **Hits:** 15
> **Total Bases:** 34
> **RBI:** 14

BULLPEN BLAZERS

1 This lefty was the first Redbird in history to appear in over half his club's games, as he led the majors with 89 outings while posting a neat 1.80 ERA with nine saves in 10 tries. Single, plus a RBI for the year.

2 The first NL reliever to win 10 games in a season without recording a single save was this Cards righty who went 10–4 in 59 appearances for one of Torre's crews. After adding 73 more outings the next year, he moved to Florida, where he appeared in the Marlins' inaugural regular season game. Double.

3 In 1942 Howie Krist came out of the Cards pen to finish a club-high 16 games. What right-hander who finished just 12 games led the 1942 world champs with five saves, as he struck a perfect balance in his 38 appearances with 19 starts and 19 games out of the pen? Two-run triple for this often forgotten 1930s and 1940s slabster who posted 143 career wins to go with his 48 lifetime saves.

4 You can bank a three-run triple for the name of the former Pirates starter who held the Cards club record prior to NL expansion in 1962 for the most career appearances by a southpaw, all of which were made in relief.

5 In his first Cards season after arriving from an AL division winner, he became the initial Redbirds chucker (minimum 100 innings) to average more than a strikeout per inning. Working all but two of his 72 outings from the pen, he whiffed 130 in $106\frac{1}{3}$ frames and saved 11 while charting a neat 2.79 ERA. Last seen with the Birds in 1982, he was finished in the show before age 30. RBI double.

6 Name the Deadball Era southpaw who either paced or tied for the NL lead in saves three times, including twice as a Cardinal, in the process of winning 174 games. His lone 20-win season came with the first World Championship team to represent a certain NL city. Three bases for him, a RBI for his Series winner.

7 What Card's potential string of three consecutive NL save crowns did NL MVP Jim Konstanty interrupt in 1950? Double.

8 In 1939 the Cards unveiled a rookie hurler who not only tied for the club lead in saves with nine but also made 15 starts and crafted a neat 13–5 record. Need we add that he never again matched his yearling credentials? Two-run home run.

9 The first Cards hurler to make as many as 50 relief appearances in a season came out of the pen 51 times and, in addition, made two starts for a loop-leading 53 games in all. He also paced the NL in hill outings the following year with 54 but on this occasion logged 19 starts and 13 complete games. Nicknamed "Hardrock," he was born and died in Mountain City, Tenn. Put a name to our description and wallop a solo homer, plus an extra RBI for his two big pen years with the Cards.

10 The Cards pitching staff in 1958 was not used in the customary manner for that era. Both the club leader and the runner-up to him in saves qualified for the ERA title, as each made at least 20 starts and 20 relief appearances in the course of the season. The two are well-known figures from that period. One came to the team early in the 1958 season in a trade with the Cubs, for whom he had been primarily a starter, and the other later quit the game when he learned he was slated to be tethered to a 1969 NL expansion team. Name both for a RBI double; a sac hit if you know just one.

11 Better remembered for his antics than his mound work, this Cards lefty tied for the NL lead by notching 22 saves one year and in the process equaled the club mark for relief wins with 13. Snag a single for this colorful loon, a RBI for the year, and an extra base for knowing the reliever whose team victory mark he tied.

12 Look no farther than this flamethrower to find the first Cards fireman to log three straight 30-save seasons. An elbow operation followed by rotator cuff surgery shelved him for two years, but he was still productive thereafter with another NL outfit. Single, plus a RBI for nailing his three-year 30-save spread.

13 Which of these pre-expansion hurlers was the only one to log more saves than wins as a Cardinal? Clyde Shoun, Hi Bell, Syl Johnson, Jim Lindsey, Billy Muffett, Gerry Staley. Double.

14 What Hall of Famer, already past age 40, totaled at least 30 saves in each of his two seasons in Busch Stadium? Rates a bloop single, but add a RBI for his two-year stretch.

15 He came to the Cards from Milwaukee in 1958, the owner of a perfect 5–0 career record over the course of five seasons spent entirely in relief roles. Although he racked up a 5–1 mark in 1958 with a 3.56 ERA and finished a club-high 22 games in his 46 pen appearances, the Cards opted to cut him loose. Hence he left the show at age 28 with a 10–1 career log in 95 games, all in relief. Upon his departure, he possessed two career records: the most appearances by a retired NL hurler, all in relief (since broken), and the highest career winning percentage by any pitcher in NL or AL history who notched a minimum of 10 decisions (.909). The latter record still stands. Name this one-year Cards bullpen wonder and win a two-run homer.

AB: 15
Hits: 15
Total Bases: 35
RBI: 18

INNING 5
GOLD GLOVE GOLIATHS

1 No other gardener totaled more chances than this Cards performer the year he fielded a flawless 1.000. What's more, he bagged his fourth of what would be seven straight Gold Glove Awards that year. The Redbirds record holder for career outfield putouts, he's worth one base, plus a RBI for his perfect year in the pasture.

2 The first performer to play as many as 1,000 games in the pasture for the Cardinals franchise never played any position but the outfield in his 15-year career and owned the most lifetime outfield assists (122) of any Cards NL performer at the time of his retirement. He finished with the 1929 Boston Braves, and you'll finish with a two-run double if you know him.

3 The first Redbirds second sacker to earn leather bullion did it two straight years and led the NL in FA twice with the Cards. Name him for a single, plus a RBI for pegging his two award-winning seasons.

4 Lou Brock was the most recent gardener to bag as many as 100 career assists in a St. Louis uniform. Who was the first pastureman to accomplish this feat? A member of the franchise's first pennant winner, he played just four years in St. Loo and logged 123 assists in just 339 outfield games. How'd he get so many in so few contests? A lot of his assists came from playing shallow in right field and throwing runners out at first base on what today would be line-drive singles. Triple.

5 The first gardener in ML history to post a season FA as high as .950 while serving as a regular wore a St. Louis uniform. Some students of baseball's infant days consider him to have been the best center fielder ever to represent a Mound City team even though he played only three seasons in St. Loo. Double.

6 Prior to the arrival of Keith Hernandez, three first basemen compiled 110 or more assists in a season wearing St. Louis NL threads. Each member of the trio achieved his biggest glove season when the schedule still called for only 154 games. Two of the three, Ed Konetchy and Ripper Collins, were not only slick fielders but also rank among the Cards' best hitting first basemen in the pre-expansion era. But the third man, and the one who held the club season first-sack assist record prior to Hernandez, was a slew foot—he never stole a base in Cards gear—and so erratic a hitter that his .246 career BA still ranks dead last among all gateway guardians with a minimum of 800 plate appearances as a Bird. Earn your sergeant's stripes here in the form of a two-run homer.

7 This gift single comes festooned with garlands and streamers. Name the man who won the most Gold Gloves in a Cards uniform. Add a RBI for recalling his total with the Birds.

8 In 1947 this fleet-footed and sure-gloved Cards gardener became the first performer in ML history to play 100 games in a season while collecting fewer than 100 AB. RBI triple for this often-used defensive replacement who was born in St. Louis and returned from the minors to become the first centerfield regular for the AL club that had represented St. Louis prior to 1954.

9 The initial Cards hurler to earn a Gold Glove actually began the year with the Astros and then grabbed the award again the following season during his first full campaign in Birds wear. Two years earlier, this same twirler became the first performer to win Gold Gloves in both leagues, regardless of position. That clue alone lowers this to a RBI single, plus an extra ribby for knowing his first year in Cards threads.

10 The first Cards catcher to bag a Gold Glove earned three altogether while setting a ML record (since broken) for the highest season FA by a backstop in a minimum of 125 games behind the dish. Single.

11 This Redbird broke our previous performer's season record by becoming the first catcher to work a minimum of 125 games and field a perfect 1.000. Yes, he snagged the Gold Glove that year and in three other campaigns as well. Single, plus a RBI for pegging his flawless year in the field.

12 Who was the first Cardinals pitcher subsequent to Bob Gibson to earn leather ingot honors? That year he also topped the Cards in every major pitching category, so we can't offer more than a single, but add a RBI for the year.

13 He currently owns the Cards franchise's top four seasons in assists at his position and earned leather bullion honors in two of those seasons, with one of them coming on a Birds flag bearer. Double, plus a RBI for the year he did it with a pennant winner.

14 End with a three-run homer by identifying the only performer to date who played as many as 200 games in the field with the Cards during his career and never made an error. Your clues are that he booted one as a rookie with the 1997 Indians and that, in addition to fielding a perfect 1.000 while a Card, he batted .400.

AB: 14
Hits: 14
Total Bases: 27
RBI: 15

INNING 6
SHELL-SHOCKED SLINGERS

1 He holds the Cards franchise record for the highest ERA by a qualifier (6.72). Not content to leave St. Louis fans holding their

nose for just that one year, he returned the following season to post the second-highest ERA in franchise history by a qualifier (6.49). No relation to a later-day secretary of state, he is in fact the only player to date in ML history to bear his last name. Three-run homer, plus an extra RBI for his two awful seasons.

2 Ten years after earning a complete-game World Series victory against the Cards, he posted a deplorable 2–12 slate as a Redbirds starter with an ERA approaching 6.00. A former ace with another NL club, this lefty's career was decimated by injuries. RBI single, plus an extra base for his dreadful year.

3 What Hall of Famer holds the Cards mark for the highest season ERA by a qualifier with a winning record? His 13–10 log with a 5.70 ERA came on the heels of a 20-win season for a flag winner. Double for him, plus a RBI for the year.

4 One of this slabster's years was so bad that you have to read the numbers twice to comprehend them. In 107⅓ innings he yielded a staggering 30 homers, set the club season mark for most baserunners allowed per nine among hurlers with at least 15 starts (15.85), and posted an obscene 7.38 ERA. Yet somehow this 6'6" righty finished with a 7–7 record. Hard as it may be to imagine, five years earlier he had topped the Cards with 18 victories, placing second in the NL overall. Single, plus a RBI for the year his career hit rock bottom.

5 What pitcher with 119 career victories and a stellar .657 career winning percentage that included a season in which he was a MVP runner-up finished his ML days with the 1958 Cards by being blasted for 14 homers in just 53 innings of work? Double.

6 Relievers so heavily battered that opposing hitters rap .300+ against their slants seldom have productive seasons. What Cards bullpenner, in addition to being pounded for a .305 BA, gave up 11 homers in 94⅓ innings of work but nonetheless led the club in saves with nine and in winning percentage (.625) as he went 10–6 in 55 pen appearances for the first Cards club that Johnny Keane piloted? Enough meat there to rack up a RBI double for the hurler, plus an extra base for the year.

7 What Mound City native holds both the Cards' all-time season record (27) and the club's post-1900 season mark (18) for the most hit batsmen? A 27-game loser in 1897 when he set the team's all-time standard, he won 21 for the 1903 St. Louis Browns and bore a nickname that reflected his 5'7" stature. RBI triple

8 In his lone Cards season he went 10–9 as a starter-reliever while getting racked for 20 homers in 124⅓ frames and posting a 5.79 ERA, more than two runs above the league average. Three years earlier with another NL outfit, he earned 23 victories while leading in winning percentage before his career went south. Double, plus a RBI for his lousy lone Mound City season.

9 In his sophomore year, he set the Cards franchise's all-time season record for the most wild pitches with 33. The following year he set the franchise's season mark for the most walks with 232. In addition, he surrendered the most home runs of any pitcher in his loop in the course of those two seasons. With all that working against him, he *still* won 60 games over that two-year span and later posted his 200th career victory before he reached his 30th birthday. Two-run triple.

10 This Cards chucker topped the NL with 19 losses while becoming the first Redbirds moundsman to start at least 30 games in a season without completing a single assignment. Score a RBI single for this Dominican who was less than dandy, plus a RBI for the year.

11 Not since the 1890s has the Cards franchise featured a slab man who won 20 games in a season while posting a 4.50+ ERA. What Birds hurler came the closest since 1900 to reaching the "charmed circle" with so horrendous an ERA (4.52) when he won 18 in 1937 despite giving up 280 hits and 32 homers? It was a typical year for him in that he averaged nearly 18 wins in the 11 seasons he was an ERA qualifier but otherwise completely out of character, as his career ERA was 3.18 during a span when the NL average was 3.79. Take two even after receiving the tasty clue that he once won an ERA crown with another NL club.

12 After a fine 20–11 season on a Cards flag winner, he plummeted to 6–15 while posting a frightening 5.21 ERA, the worst among NL qualifiers. Dealt during the following campaign, this lefty lasted 11 more years but never regained his halcyon form. RBI single, plus an extra base for the year he bagged 20 wins.

13 Another well-traveled southpaw was this Glen Falls, N.Y., product who averaged 13.30 baserunners per nine innings, the worst career mark by a Cards hurler (minimum 500 innings) since WWII. Nonetheless, his lifetime Redbirds slate was 35–23 and included consecutive 12-win seasons in which he finished over .500 in both campaigns. One of four men the Birds received in that blockbuster deal that sent Vuckovich, Simmons, and Fingers to Milwaukee, he's good for two.

14 1910 brought the ML debut of a stocky 24-year-old righty nicknamed "Big Bill" who logged a 4–4 record and a 3.27 ERA that was to be his highwater mark in a five-year career that finished with him ranking the worst of all the Cards Deadball Era (1901–1919) hurlers who worked a minimum of 500 innings with the club. Big Bill stood dead last in ERA (3.98), last in hits allowed per nine innings (9.76), and last in baserunners allowed per nine innings (13.27) before moving on near the end of the 1914 season to Brooklyn where he concluded his ML tour. Granted, none of Big Bill's composite stats for his days with the Cards would seem particularly shabby today, but in his time he was one heavily battered Bird. Stand up to this test of your mettle and win a home run.

15 This duo truly befouled the Cards' hill stats one recent season as one lost a NL-leading 17 games while posting a 5.70 ERA. His partner in crime was even more heinous going an execrable 2–14 with a 6.04 ERA. Score a single but only if you nail both terrible tossers.

AB: 15
Hits: 15
Total Bases: 34
RBI: 16

INNING 7
HEROES AND GOATS

1 A true fall hero, to date he's the only moundsman other than Christy Mathewson to start three games in three different World Series. Since he's a Cardinal, he won't net more than a bloop single.

2 After 1946 World Series hero Harry Brecheen notched a route-going win in Game 6, what unexpected aid did he receive that helped him to win Game 7? Two baser.

3 Handcuffed by Royals pitching, the Cards batted just .185 during their loss in the 1985 World Series. This Redbird goat was the worst of the bunch, managing just two measly singles in 23 at bats while committing a rare throwing error that led to a Royals run. Single.

4 Brooklyn's Don Newcombe lost all four of his World Series decisions to the Yanks. But earlier a Cards lefty showed Newk the way by dropping all four of his Fall Classic starts against the Bombers, including what proved to be a Series clincher one year. Triple.

5 Mickey Mantle unloaded his record-breaking 16th Fall Classic homer in the last of the ninth on the first offering from a certain Cards knuckleballer to give the Yanks a 2–1 victory in Game 2 of the 1964 Series. The Mick's victim went on to post a horrendous 18.00 ERA for his four fall bullpen appearances after being one of the Cards' main heroes during the regular season. Two bases.

6 What hurler led the NL in winning percentage when he became an instant hero by garnering his 15th victory against just six losses in the second game of the pennant playoff series with the Dodgers to clinch the 1946 pennant for the Cards? RBI double.

7 The Cards advanced to the 1985 Series after defeating the Dodgers in Games 5 and 6 of the NLCS due to ninth-inning homers by two different players. Name both of these clutch-dinger heroes and earn a single, zip for just one. However, you can add an extra base for nailing the beleaguered LA reliever who yielded each blast.

8 Stationed in center field for most of the regular season, this Redbird hit an even .300. But in fall play that year he slipped a certain opponent a mickey and added insult to injury by leading all Series performers in just about every major batting department when he hit .500 in a seven-game fray. His name rates a single and the opponent he made a fall goat merits a ribby.

9 What reigning bat titlist was considered the goat of a St. Louis ML team's first ever postseason loss when he compiled a World Series batting average that was 235 points below his regular season BA? Single for the hitter; two ribbies for his season BA that year.

10 When the Redbirds won the 1964 Series, it spared this rookie reliever from being labeled a goat for surrendering two runs in Game 2 and yielding a grand slam to the first batter he faced (Joe Pepitone) in Game 6, tagging him with a not-so-nifty 40.50 ERA for his Series efforts. Dealt that winter to the lowly Mets, he appeared in 50 games with the New Yorkers over the next two years before leaving the bigs. Believe it or not, we think this Georgia southpaw merits a two-run shot.

11 He remains the only performer to this day on a Cards flag winner to top the Birds in batting average and lead the entire NL in slugging average, OPS, extra base hits, and home runs. Rather amazingly, his heroic year was the only one in which he collected black ink in a batting department. Two-run double, plus an extra base for his super season.

12 We won't insult you by asking what Hall of Famer came out of the pen to fan Tony Lazzeri and shut the Yanks down cold to ice the Cards' first world title representing the NL in 1926. But you do have to know who shared the hero's mantle with him that day by gaining credit for the win. RBI double.

13 After hitting a club-record .314 during the regular season, the Cards plummeted to just .200 in their 1930 World Series loss to the A's. What slugger epitomized the Cards' fall woes and earned goat horns by batting just .045 and fanning nine times in 22 at bats? Two-bagger.

14 Notoriously feeble at the plate, he offset his offensive woes in the Mound City with fine leatherwork. However, he really out-did himself one fall by setting the ML record for most at bats in a World Series (22) without stroking a single hit. The Cards lost in seven that year, but you can win a RBI single for him, plus an extra base for the year.

15 Many Cards fans will always believe that first base umpire Don Denkinger was the goat of the 1985 World Series for declaring Royals pinch hitter Jorge Orta safe on first sacker Jack Clark's toss to pitcher Todd Worrell to lead off the bottom of the ninth in Game 6. More impartial observers contend that Clark was the real goat for failing to snag a catchable pop foul by the next Kansas City batter that landed near the Cards dugout. That hit-ter then singled to trigger a two-run rally that gave Kansas City a last-ditch 2–1 win. Making his hit all the harder for St. Louisans to stomach even today is the knowledge that he finished his ML career in 1993 with a .229 BA in 960 games, all in the junior cir-cuit. Who was the Royal that Clark's foul-pop faux pas spared to hit safely? Double.

AB: 15
Hits: 15
Total Bases: 29
RBI: 10

WHAT WAS THEIR REAL HANDLE?

1 Von McDaniel. Home run.

2 Cy Young. RBI single.

3 Mickey Owen. RBI double.

4 Shorty Fuller. Three-run homer.

5 Debs Garms. Triple.

6 Mike Shannon. RBI double.

7 Red Munger. Double.

8 Bud Byerly. Two-run triple.

9 Whitey Herzog. It's been tossed around a lot, so just a single.

10 Tex Carleton. Triple.

11 Flint Rhem. Two-run triple.

12 Bo Hart. Triple.

13 Red Murray. Homer.

14 Bugs Raymond. Three-run triple.

15 Bruno Betzel. Grand slam.

AB: 15
Hits: 15
Total Bases: 42
RBI: 19

INNING 9
FALL CLASSICS

1 Only he can make the following claim: I both homered and managed in Series play wearing a Cardinals NL uniform. Triple.

2 Although he didn't debut until June of that season, this Cards frosh earned the complete-game victory in October that sent the Birds to a seventh game and ultimately a World Championship. Winner of just 32 career games, he'll wake you from your daze and send you to second, plus a RBI for the year of his freshman feat.

3 In what year did these names appear on the Cards' roster of eligible players for the World Series? Bill Endicott, Walt Sessi, and Jeff Cross. Solo homer, plus two extra RBI if you know the special circumstances that enabled them to accrue Series money.

4 When Brooklyn started southpaw Joe Hatten in the second and deciding game of the 1946 NL pennant playoff series, the Cards sat Harry Walker and installed the right-handed hitting half of their leftfield platoon in the sixth slot in the batting order. Before being replaced by Walker when the Dodgers changed to a right-hander late in the game, he went 2-for-3, including a triple, and bore a nickname that rhymed with his last name. Two-run triple.

5 In 1968 Roger Maris started five of the seven Series contests in right field for the Cards while a backup gardener the Birds acquired from the Astros in June patrolled that spot in Games 2 and 5. Even after being armed with the knowledge that his name matches that of a future reliever who saved 130 games from 1978 to 1988, you deserve a triple for this forgotten sub.

6 Commissioner Landis ordered Joe Medwick to be removed from the seventh and deciding game of the 1934 World Series when Detroit fans pelted Medwick with bottles and garbage after he slid hard into the Tigers third baseman in the sixth inning. Name the Motor City third sacker for a double, plus two RBI for the Card who subbed for Medwick after he left the game.

7 In 1926 Pete Alexander notched two complete-game wins and a Game 7 save in three Series outings for the Cards. What Birds hurler matched his feat and then some in the 1931 Fall Classic when he posted a shutout and a 0.49 ERA to go with his two complete-game wins and Game 7 save? Two-run single.

8 Who is the only Card to capture the NLCS and World Series MVP in the same postseason? Although he smote .556 during the playoffs, his Series numbers (.286 BA, 1 HR, 5 RBI) failed to top the Birds in any of those categories. Two-base hit.

9 Name the Redbird who boasts the worst regular season ERA (5.76) of any starting pitcher to win a deciding Fall Classic contest. Incredibly, he *lowered* his composite ERA as a Card after posting a 6.29 figure and a 3–10 slate with his previous club that released him in favor of his younger brother. He was the only Birds slinger to start two Series games that year, and you should rap him for a single.

10 Despite leading a World Champion Cards club with a crisp .421 BA and a team-best five runs in a certain Fall Classic, this infielder failed to earn Series MVP honors. What's more, the Cards catcher was second to him on the team at .412 and was also denied the top prize. Double for both, scratch single for one, plus add a RBI for the year.

11 What hurler was the beneficiary of the Cards' greatest post-season hit parade to date when his mates rained 20 safeties in his support, enabling him to top the Red Sox 12–3 in Game 4 of the 1946 World Series? RBI double.

12 Gibson and Brock deservedly hogged the headlines during the 1967 Series, but it might surprise you which of their team-mates stroked .385 during that clash and led both clubs with seven RBI. We'll wager a double that he slips under your radar.

13 When the Cards appeared in a twentieth-century World Series for the first time in 1926, who was the only club member that had previously seen postseason action? His initial taste of fall ball came under the direction of John McGraw, and his final nibble of October frenzy saw him acting as one of the directors himself. Name the man who smote .345 for the 1926 champs for a RBI double, plus another RBI for his final fall appearance.

14 What performer who debuted with the 1946 Cardinals is one of the only two multiyear players in ML history to play on a World Series winner in both their first and last seasons in the majors? Polish off a home run for him, plus a RBI for the club with which he finished his career, and a second RBI for the performer with whom he shares this estimable distinction.

AB: 14
Hits: 14
Total Bases: 33
RBI: 17

GAME 7

INNING 1
RBI RULERS

1 From 1958 to 1964 Ken Boyer topped the Cards in RBI every year except one. Who snuck in that year with 102 ribbies to deny Boyer seven straight team-leader crowns? Double.

2 What Card was the first NLer since Dixie Walker in 1946 to rack up a 100 RBI season in which he poked fewer than 10 taters? A switch-hitter, he plated 110 runs while popping just eight jacks the year after he pushed across a mere 49 mates in 558 at bats. RBI single, plus an extra sack for his one-of-a-kind big ribby season.

3 After Joe Torre in 1971 it would be over 20 years before another Cards third baseman pushed across 100 runners. This swinger shared something else with Torre beyond the fact that he batted from the right side and collected over 200 career homers. Two for his name, plus a RBI for the distinction he shared with Joe.

4 In his first year in Cards garb he paced the club with 108 RBI while setting the current team record by fanning 167 times. The following season he plated 110, and surpassed that total three years later with the Birds. Single.

5 The Cards franchise once had a catcher who bagged 76 RBI in just 72 games. In addition, he hit .366 that year and had a .636 SA. Why didn't he play more? It's a question St. Loo fans asked loud and often at the end of that season, as their team finished a close second to Brooklyn. Sounds a bit like 1940, but it was long before then. Name the receiver for a home run, plus his big year for two extra RBI.

6 Who posted the lowest season RBI total (44) of any Cards club ribby leader to date? At that, he played just 87 games that year. Even with the clue that he's in the Hall of Fame, this is still a triple, plus three RBI if you also know the year involved.

7 Who drew the fewest walks for a St. Louis NL entry during a 100 RBI season? Another Cooperstown-bound swinger comes your way in this performer who coaxed just 21 free passes coupled with 106 RBI for a Birds pennant winner. Double, plus a RBI for the year.

8 Rogers Hornsby set a new Cards franchise RBI record in 1921 when he banged home 126 runners. What year did Hornsby first top the NL in RBI? Triple.

9 In 1930, the Cards scored a post-1892 club-record 1,004 runs. Who led the team in RBI that year with a rather modest total of 114? RBI double.

10 Which one of these players never led a Cardinals club in RBI? Tom Brunansky, Ray Lankford, Keith Hernandez, Reggie Smith, Dick Allen, Scott Rolen. RBI single.

11 During Joe Torre's four full seasons at the Cards helm, just one performer drove in 100+ runs. Approach this teaser with enthusiasm and you just may rap a RBI single through the wickets.

12 Johnny Mize racked up five straight 100 RBI seasons with the Cards before he was traded to the Giants. Who was the next first sacker after Mize's departure to register a 100 RBI season in Redbirds garb? The clue that he was the lone Bird to log a 100 RBI campaign during the Cards' 1942–1944 pennant run will help experts to score a two-run triple here, plus a third RBI for the year.

13 What Cardinal totaled the most RBI in a season by any performer since WWII without hitting a homer? His 75 ribbies came with a Cards flag bearer and proved to be a career high for this 19-year vet. RBI single, plus an extra base for the year.

14 What member of the Gas House Gang set the current Cards club record for the most RBI in a season by a switch-hitter? Double.

AB: 14
Hits: 14
Total Bases: 30
RBI: 15

INNING 2
MVP MARVELS

1 What Card was the only player in the history of MVP voting to share the award due to a tie in that year's balloting? Single for him, a RBI for the year, plus an extra base for naming the Hall of Famer with whom this Redbird was co-honored.

2 What fly chaser, in his first season after coming to the Cards, placed second in the MVP balloting with a Redbirds world champ but never again cracked the top 10 in the voting at any other juncture in his career? RBI single.

3 The lone pitcher in NL history to date who either won or was a runner-up for MVP honors three years in a row was a Cardinal. Single for him, extra base for his three-year run.

4 What one-time NL batting champ finished second in the MVP vote during his first year with the Cards after logging nine seasons for a team with whom he had previously captured a MVP honor? RBI single, plus an extra base for the year.

5 The first backstopper ever to claim a MVP prize was a Cardinal. He beat out Cincinnati's Hughie Critz for the honor and was also the first position player to snare a MVP despite logging a sub-.300 batting average. He's a two-bagger, and his triumphant year rates another base.

6 In the only year during his lengthy ML stay that he ever received a single MVP vote, this Card placed second to a fellow

Redbird. Grab a double for the runner-up, an extra base for the winner, and a RBI for knowing the year this tandem went 1–2.

7 What Cards MVP hit just .170 with no homers and a .456 OPS during his award-winning season? Take a moment to figure out the catch here and slap an obvious single, plus a RBI for the year.

8 Stan Musial drew his first MVP votes in 1942, when he got 26. What four Cardinals finished ahead of him in the balloting that year? Need all four for a two-run triple. Single if you know only three.

9 What Card won a MVP in the lone year he received any votes? A four-time All-Star, he's also the first position player who could make this claim upon retirement. Single, plus a RBI for the year.

10 When Stan Musial won his first MVP prize in 1943, what Cardinal was runner-up to him in the voting even though he played only 122 games? Two-bagger.

11 A fractious appendix led to an off year that took Stan the Man out of the running for the 1947 NL MVP Award. Who was the only member of the defending world champs to finish in the top 10 that year in the balloting? Your clue is that he never again received a single MVP vote. RBI double.

12 The Man won his final MVP Award in 1948. Who was the only Cardinal to finish as high as second in the balloting between 1948 and NL expansion in 1962? Single.

13 Who won a MVP with the Cards but finished second the next year despite adding eight more homers and 20 more RBI to his ledger while playing in 18 fewer games? We can't in good conscience offer more than a single for this slugging star, but we'll award a charitable RBI for the year he earned the MVP.

14 Beginning with the current MVP Award's inception in 1931, the Cards enjoyed a lengthy streak when they had at least one player notch a vote. The first year no Redbirds received a single tally in the MVP race occurred in a season when the Cards dropped 93 games and posted their lowest winning percentage in 54 years. What year are we citing? Three bases.

AB: 14
Hits: 14
Total Bases: 27
RBI: 10

INNING 3
RED-HOT ROOKIES

1 Identify this Swift Current, Saskatchewan, native who led yearling senior-loop tossers with 12 victories and tied for top-circuit honors in starts (34) and complete games (10). Although named the NL Rookie Pitcher of the Year by *The Sporting News*, he garnered nary a vote from the scribes in that season's frosh balloting. Single, plus a RBI for the year.

2 In his first full season, he led NL freshmen in games, doubles, homers, RBI, and slugging. However, it was a lean year for rookie sticks, and his .625 OPS was the lowest in the majors among third sackers who totaled at least 500 plate appearances. Just 23 at the time, this Puerto Rico native never played regularly again. RBI single, plus an extra base for the season in question.

3 After getting a brief glance from the wretched Cleveland Spiders in 1899 and St. Louis the following year, this third sacker tied for the NL lead in games played in the first year of the new century, which coincided with his official rookie year. But, alas, after his promising beginning, the man nicknamed "Oom Paul" enjoyed only one more season as a regular before drifting into utility roles for the remaining three years of his career. Name the

Cards' first rookie sensation in the twentieth century, after receiving the clue that he was a bust thereafter, and collect a three-run homer.

4 After he'd gone an insipid 7-for-59 (.119) in two brief earlier trials, he was given his first real shot by the Birds and responded with a .301 BA while topping NL frosh in games, doubles, walks, and runs. An infielder all the way, he later served as a regular on a Cardinals flag winner before closing with the Angels in 1992. Double, plus a RBI for his big frosh year.

5 In 1912 this Cards gardener led all NL rookie qualifiers with a .290 BA. Seven years later, by then with the Cubs, he was rudely notified that he had played his last ML game when NL clubs combined to ban him unofficially for gambling and game fixing. RBI triple for the man who entered this world as Leopold Hoernschemeyer.

6 One year a 23-year-old fly chaser led ML freshmen with eight triples, stole 24 bags, and hit .296 in 123 games for a Cards flag bearer. None of those figures would be career highs, as he played on three Cards pennant winners all told and finished his career at age 40 with the Redbirds. Single, plus a RBI for his rookie year.

7 Catchers who don't reach the majors until they're over 30 generally have glaring offensive deficiencies. What Cards fledgling receiver was the notable exception, pounding NL hurlers for a .565 slugging average and a .979 OPS as a 32-year-old freshman with the Gas House Gang? Two bases for him, RBI for the year.

8 Tom Seaver crowded out several fine arms for NL Rookie of the Year honors, including this former Razorback who topped the Cards in wins with 16 while leading the senior circuit, rookie or no, with a .727 winning percentage. As swiftly as he cometed to stardom, he descended, so catch this falling star for a double.

9 A successful late-season trial in 1906 led to him being installed as the Cards mound ace the following spring. He responded with 14 wins and 33 complete games as a 35-year-old frosh in what was to be his only full season in the majors. A rocky road is ahead of you if you don't score a solo homer here.

10 A brief taste of the bigs with the 1938 Reds was all this 33-year-old perennial minor leaguer had to boast about until the spring of 1948, when he suddenly was handed the Cards' third base slot by default after Whitey Kurowski was unable to answer the bell. In 117 games as a rook, he stroked .269. Stroke a three-run homer if you can dredge up his name.

11 In his first ML appearance at age 24, he tossed a complete-game shutout, and in his second ML start was about to join the select group of hurlers who have debuted with two straight white-washings when Solly Hemus made an error with two away in the ninth, allowing an unearned run that ruined our man's bid for a second shutout. Unlike many of the ephemeral yearling chuckers the Cards have unveiled, this performer toiled until age 40, logging over 700 big league appearances. Double, plus a RBI for his rookie season.

12 A product of Branch Rickey's Byzantine farm system, he tied for the overall NL lead in games played as a Cards frosh with 153 in 1925 while pacing senior-circuit rooks in at bats, hits, doubles, runs, RBI, and walks. After striking .325 as a soph for the 1926 world champs, he tailed off, and by 1928 he was dealt to the Braves, where he failed to play regularly after age 27. RBI double.

13 This 29-year-old rook didn't make his debut for the Cards until nearly midseason but nevertheless went 15–6 and led the club with a .714 winning percentage to take the sting out of the disappointing year that winter trade acquisition Vic Raschi produced. Link those clues to nail the rook for a triple, plus a RBI for the year.

14 In his rookie season he was the only member of the Cards to play in as many as 100 games or qualify for the NL batting title. His 156 hits were 67 more than the number produced by the runner-up for team honors, Al Burch (who was also a rookie). In addition, our mystery man placed second to Miller Huggins for the major league lead in assists among players at his position. But after playing 82 games the following year and hitting a paltry .222, he disappeared forever from the majors. Name this long-forgotten red-hot fledgling whose real first name was Justin for a two-run homer, plus an extra RBI for the year he debuted.

AB: 14
Hits: 14
Total Bases: 36
RBI: 19

INNING 4
WHO'D THEY COME UP WITH?

Remember, knowing the year in which each of these Cards made his big league debut will earn you two extra RBI.

1 Pete Alexander. Just a single.

2 Jason Isringhausen. Single.

3 Bob O'Farrell. RBI double.

4 "Toothpick" Sam Jones. Triple.

5 Scott Spiezio. Single.

6 Roger Bresnahan. Two-run homer.

7 George Crowe. RBI triple.

8 George Hendrick. Double.

9 Charles "Red" Barrett. Two-run homer.

10 Coaker Triplett. Three-run circuit blast.

11 Jim Edmonds. Bunt single.

12 Darrell Porter. Single.

13 Bill Doak. Homer.

14 Fernando Vina. RBI double.

15 Debs Garms. Two-run homer.

AB: 15
Hits: 15
Total Bases: 37
RBI: 43

INNING 5
STRIKEOUT KINGS

1 Bob Gibson—who else?—dominates the Cardinals' season and career strikeout leader list. However, you can tally a two-run triple by naming the franchise's record holder for the most whiffs in a season by a lefty. Take an extra ribby for knowing the year he blew the opposition away and special pride in nailing a question that is much tougher than it might seem at a glance.

2 Dating all the way back to the Cardinals' ancestral predecessor—the 1882 Browns—who was the first member of the Cards franchise to win a loop strikeout crown? Take the clues that he debuted in 1889 and pitched on several great Boston teams in the 1890s and race to a two-run triple.

3 Who was the first Cards chucker following Bob Gibson's retirement to fan at least 100 batters in five straight seasons? Single, plus a RBI for his five-year run.

4 Name the southpaw who copped the first two of what became a string of six straight strikeout crowns won by Cards pitchers when we tell you the Birds' lengthy K reign happened between 1920 and 1942. RBI two-bagger.

5 The most recent Redbird moundsman to lead the NL in strikeouts is also the most recent Cards flinger to fan 200 batters in consecutive seasons. This forkball practitioner possessed great stuff but never really put it all together and fell apart soon thereafter. RBI single for him, plus an extra base for the year he topped the NL in whiffs.

6 He was both the first hurler to win a loop strikeout crown after spending his triumphant season with two different teams and the first Cardinals tosser to pace the NL in Ks. A rookie no less, he came to St. Louis in a trade for Jack Taylor and led the club in wins, albeit with a mere nine, despite not being acquired until July. He rates a two-run homer, plus another ribby for his triumphant year.

7 Only once in a season in which Bob Gibson started at least 30 games did another Redbird top the club in whiffs. That season our mystery moundsman also paced the Birds in wins (16), led all Cards qualifiers in ERA (2.69), and toiled in the All-Star Game. Double for him, plus a RBI for the year he bested Gibby in Ks.

8 Excepting the 1981 strike season, the most recent hurler to win a ML loop strikeout crown with fewer than 150 Ks was a Cardinal. His winning total was 149, and it was not only his personal high but also one of the only two seasons in his 12-year career in which his whiff total reached triple digits. This improbable K king's name and the year he won the crown are worth a double, but you need both to score.

9 Who currently is the only hurler other than Bob Gibson to fan 1,000 batters in Redbirds raiment since WWII? More amazingly, he never whiffed more than 114 in any one season, clueing you that this chucker lasted a while in the Mound City. Double.

10 Prior to Bob Gibson's arrival in 1959, Dizzy Dean headed the list of Cardinals career pitching strikeout leaders with 1,095. What hurler was second on the list with 979? RBI double.

11 Although not generally considered a whiff master, his 213 punch-outs one season were the most by a Cards hurler in 35 years, placing him second in the NL, just three behind the loop leader. Just a single, but add a RBI for the year.

12 The Birds have never had a portsider on the order of a Sandy Koufax or a Randy Johnson. Yet no fewer than eight of the 13 twirlers on the Cards' top baker's dozen list in career pitching strikeouts prior to Bob Gibson's arrival in 1959 were southpaws. Name all eight for a two-run homer. Double for five or more. Zip for less.

13 The first St. Louis NL hurler to fan as many as 200 batters in a season after the present pitching distance was set in 1893 wasn't born when the rubber was first laid 60'6" from the plate and was just seven years old the year Dizzy Dean set the club season record of 199 that he broke. Who is he for a deuce?

14 Which one of these tossers never fanned as many as 175 batters in a season with the Redbirds? Todd Stottlemyre, Ernie Broglio, Darryl Kile, Andy Benes, John Tudor, Matt Morris. Single.

15 The first rookie to lead the Cards in Ks after the mound was set at its present distance is in the Hall of Fame. He had all of 83 whiffs the year he achieved this freshman first in team annals, and you should know us well enough by now not to be surprised by our clue that after his frosh season he never logged another strikeout in Cards livery. End on a three-bagger, plus a RBI for his leadership year.

AB: 15
Hits: 15
Total Bases: 34
RBI: 16

INNING 6
STELLAR STICKWIELDERS

1 Four switch-hitters (minimum 500 PA) have had seasons in Cards red in which they hit .340 or better. Who was the first of this quartet to do it? Double for him, plus a RBI for his breakthrough .346 season.

2 Between Stan the Man in 1952 and Big Mac in 1998, only one other Cards performer led the NL in slugging. He pounded a .597 SA on a Birds flag bearer before exiting the Mound City as a free agent. RBI single.

3 Who is the only Cardinal before the expansion era to rap 200 hits twice without making the Hall of Fame? He did it in consecutive seasons, with the second year coming for a Birds flag winner that faced the Mackmen in the Series. We doubt you'll double here.

4 Who was the first player born outside the United States to win a batting crown with a St. Louis NL club? Sure-bet single.

5 In 1927 the Cards unveiled a rookie backup catcher who logged a .994 OPS despite batting just .288. His 47 walks that year still stand as the club record for the most free passes by a player with less than 200 at bats. Something of a "one-year wonder," he never again did anything noteworthy in the majors, but you can do yourself proud by nailing a grand-slam homer here.

6 He became the first Cardinal (besides Stan Musial, who did it three times) to hit .300 while drawing as many as 100 walks. Unlike Musial, however, he fanned 150 times in his triple-digit walk season. Single, plus a RBI for the year.

7 Who was the only Cardinal to lead the NL in runs scored a minimum of three straight years? Moreover, he and Pete Rose are the only NL performers to reign outright for that long in runs since 1900. RBI single.

8 When Rogers Hornsby collected his 1,558th career-total base, what big tipper's old franchise record of 1,557 did he break? Double.

9 Who was the first batting-title qualifier subsequent to NL expansion in 1962 to stroke .325 or better in consecutive seasons in a Cards uniform? In his six seasons in Birds threads, those were the only two campaigns in which he hit .300. RBI single, plus an extra base for his two-year run.

10 The 1931 NL batting race was the closest three-way bat-title chase in ML history. A Card won by a fraction of a point, and another Redbird finished third, just one percentage point back. Can you name them and also the hitter who finished in between them in their order of finish? RBI double if all players and their order are correct. Single if you know only the two Redbirds.

11 Just one batsman to date has led the National League in triples three straight years. He paced the senior loop with totals of 18, 13, and 19, respectively, during the only seasons of his 16-year career that he reached double figures in three-baggers. RBI single, plus an extra base for his three leadership seasons.

12 In 1895, his first season as a St. Louis regular, he snared 264 total bases to become the first member of a NL Mound City club to top 250 in a season. In addition, he slapped .342. Get off your posterior and zap the man teammates called Dick for a homer, after our clue that he finished his career in 1905 and was displaced in center field by a rookie named Tyrus Cobb.

13 The year he set the Cardinals season mark for most at bats (586) without stroking a triple, he hit .287 with 37 doubles on a Redbirds flag bearer. During the previous campaign, he poked just one three-bagger in 587 at bats and slammed 47 two-baggers to set a club record for doubles at his position. Name him for a single, plus a RBI for the year he failed to stroke a trey.

14 In 1894 the NL as a whole hit a record .310. Who led the St. Louis entry that year with a .339 figure? His real name was

George, but teammates knew him by a variety of other names. Three-bagger.

15 Rumor has it that Rogers Hornsby at one time held the Cards franchise season record for the most total bases by a shortstop. Is that rumor true? If not, why isn't it? Double.

> **AB:** 15
> **Hits:** 15
> **Total Bases:** 30
> **RBI:** 13

INNING 7
HOME RUN KINGS

1 The only player in Cards history to rap as many as 30 homers in a season and total fewer strikeouts than taters struck the seats 39 times in his big year while collecting just 34 whiffs. The following year he went deep 36 times with just 38 Ks. He nets only a single, but add two extra bases if you identify the two years we're highlighting.

2 Here's one for the numerologists. What Cardinal belted exactly 24 home runs in four straight seasons? Adding that he had three other campaigns in which he hit more than 24 jacks in a Birds suit makes this a RBI single, plus an extra base for his odd four-year streak.

3 The Cards have always had good gap hitters. Consequently, only one Redbird performer prior to NL expansion in 1962 ever hammered as many as 20 dingers in a season without hitting any triples. He rapped 20 taters on the nose to go with 101 RBI for the only St. Louis NL team to date that had a shot at winning four straight pennants. Homer for him, plus a bonus RBI for the year.

4 Whose club record did Albert Pujols first break in 2003 for the most home runs in a season that also included 50 or more doubles? Single for him, two RBI for his big year.

5 Who set the current Cards team career mark for homers by a shortstop when he blasted his 35th fence climber? During his six-year stay at Busch, he more than doubled Marty Marion's former club career standard of 34. Single.

6 When he blasted 22 homers in his first year with the Cards, the Birds became the sixth NL team for which he had connected at least 20 times in a season. The next year, injuries limited him to just 93 games, but he still ripped 21 jacks before packing his bags once again, this time for the other team from Missouri. Single.

7 The first third sacker to produce a season double-digit home run total as a member of a Cards NL squad did it for the 1925 crew. Ring up a triple if you can name him.

8 Among these six players, who hit the most homers in Redbirds flannels? Ray Lankford, Mark McGwire, Rogers Hornsby, Johnny Mize, Jim Bottomley, Ted Simmons. Single.

9 Who was the Cards' first switch-hitting outfielder to drill 20 or more home runs in a season? Arriving in St. Louis from the AL, he adjusted easily, swatting 23 fence climbers and topping the club with a .917 OPS, fourth best in the loop. He played in that year's All-Star Game too, and you can etch your name on our ballot by naming him for a RBI single, plus earn an extra base for the year. Take two more RBI if you know the prior club record holder for the most dingers by a switch-stick gardener.

10 Mark McGwire pasted at least 20 jacks in each of his five seasons with the Cards. However, Big Mac was not the first Redbird gateway guardian to club 20 or more dingers for five years running. Name the man who was and earn a double, plus a RBI for knowing his five-year span.

11 What early-day St. Louis star hoisted a .691 slugging average one season despite hitting just 14 home runs? Think about this a bit and his name will be on the end of your tongue. Double.

12 Just 23 years old when he topped the 1984 Cards with 15 bombs, this righty stick never again played regularly, hanging on for parts of two seasons thereafter before departing the bigs. Show your true colors by naming him and you'll be the envy of Redbird rooters everywhere. RBI double.

13 Whose .414 career slugging average as a Card is easily the lowest among performers who drilled 100+ homers in Birds threads? Nonetheless, he notched six All-Star berths, including one in his final big league campaign. Single.

14 Can you name the only performer to log over 2,000 plate appearances with the Cards, compile a sub-.450 SA in a Birds suit, and yet register an OPS above .850 for his work in St. Loo? Double for knowing the lone Bird since Tip O'Neill to meet the career plate appearance criterion and post both a .400+ slugging average and on base percentage.

AB: 14
Hits: 14
Total Bases: 27
RBI: 10

INNING 8
MASTER MOUNDSMEN

1 Currently, two Cards ERA qualifiers have had seasons in which they limited opposing batters to an average below .200. One was Bob Gibson, who handcuffed hitters to a .184 BA in 1968. The other confounded swatters at a .197 rate, despite posting a 3.05 ERA while going 16–12 on a Herzog entry that finished third in the NL East. Double.

2 The last ML hurler to win 40 games in a season twice in his career finished his days in the show with the abysmal 1897 St. Louis NL crew, going 1–4 for a team that went 29–102. Though he was born in Connecticut and graduated from Yale, he spent most of his life in Missouri and died in Kansas City in 1926. This hard-throwing righty rates a RBI double.

3 Two Cards in the twentieth century won 20 games in consecutive seasons while logging ERAs above 3.00 in each season. The first to do it is in the Hall; the other twirler debuted in the bigs two years after the Cooperstown moundsman passed away. Triple for both, single for one.

4 Among those who notched at least 100 victories in Cards cloth since 1900, who posted the highest career winning percentage as a Redbird? Note that this Missouri native threw his last pitch for the Birds at age 32 before drifting to three other teams and reached double figures in wins just once after departing St. Louis. Double.

5 Who is the lone chucker since 1900 to win 20 games in consecutive seasons with second-division Cardinal clubs? He must have played on some pretty lousy Birds teams, right? Wrong. In fact, the Cards won three flags during this particular decade. Single for him, plus an extra base for his two seasons.

6 He collected his first ML win in relief on September 14, 1937, when the Birds beat the Phils 9–8 in the first game of a twinbill. When he returned to the Cards from World War II, his career mark stood at 37–9. Released in 1946 after he suffered two losses with no wins, he nonetheless finished with a .771 career winning percentage, the best ever among hurlers who threw a minimum of 300 innings with the Birds. In 1943, his lone season as an ERA qualifier, he logged in at 11–5 with a 2.90 ERA. Name him for a two-run triple.

7 The youngest pitcher to win an ERA crown for a St. Louis NL entry was just 22 when he posted a sparkling 1.75 figure, but he would not have snagged top honors under today's rules because he failed to work the required innings. However, in his next big league campaign he not only copped another ERA title but also led the NL with 266 innings pitched. Double for this Southern southpaw.

8 The last hurler in Cards history to complete as many as 30 games in a season scored just 17 victories in the majors, all of them with St. Louis. He's worth three bases, plus a RBI for the year he racked up 33 complete games.

9 He once had a year with the Cards in which he posted a 2.03 ERA and allowed just 9.58 enemy baserunners per nine innings and yet still managed to lose 25 games, including a record 11 in which his team was shut out. It was his only full season in St. Louis, and it came just four years before he died from head injuries he sustained in a fracas after a sandlot game. Known by the same nickname as Elmer's nemesis, he rates a triple, plus a RBI for his 25-loss season.

10 En route to his leading the NL with a 2.18 ERA, this Redbird also set the current ML record for fewest wins in a season by an ERA titlist. A southpaw, he retired with a disappointing 57–67 ledger and never qualified for another ERA title after age 29. RBI single, plus an extra base for his league-leading year.

11 RBI double if you know the three hurlers who won 20 games three or more times in a Cards NL suit prior to expansion in 1962. No credit for less.

12 What Cards lefty got off to a flying start one season by winning his first six hill appearances and throwing two shutouts, only to disappear from the majors thereafter for over three years? We'll add more ingredients to the pot. His disappearance was not the result of a military service interruption and he was last seen with the 1953 Browns. Now stir the mix and dine on a double, plus a ribby for the year he started and finished 6–0.

13 Acquired from the Blue Jays, he led Cards qualifiers with a 2.55 ERA in his first year with the club. The following season he shared the team high with 15 victories, and in his third Mound City campaign this flinger paced Birds qualifiers in ERA, plus wins. Two years later, he started two Series games *against* the Redbirds. RBI single, plus an extra ribby for the season this one-time Cy Young winner opposed the Cardinals in fall play.

14 Since Harry Brecheen notched 21 complete games in 1948, only two other Redbirds finished at least 20 starting assignments, and both did it the same season. Triple for both, single for just one, plus a RBI for the year.

> **AB:** 14
> **Hits:** 14
> **Total Bases:** 32
> **RBI:** 11

INNING 9
FALL CLASSICS

1 Dizzy and Paul Dean set the Tigers on their collective ear in the 1934 Series, bagging all four Redbirds wins and starting five of the seven contests. What two Cards hillmen started Games 2 and 4, each of which resulted in a St. Louis loss? Two bases for each, plus two RBI for the staff member who took the loss in relief in both of those contests.

2 Stroke a sure-shot single by naming the Bird who rapped 11 hits in 23 at bats to pace regulars on both sides with a .478 BA during the 1964 Series.

3 The Cards' offensive bright spot in their crushing Series loss to the Yankees in 1943 hit .357 and batted in the eighth slot. Name him. RBI double.

4 Vince Coleman missed the final three games of the 1985 NLCS and the entire World Series after an automatic tarp rolled over his leg. What Joplin, Mo., native replaced him in left and led the Birds by stroking .360 against Royals pitching in fall action, plus paced both sides with 14 total bases? Double.

5 Who was the Cards leadoff batter in the first pennant playoff game in ML history on October 1, 1946? RBI single after our clue that he led all participants in the game with seven assists.

6 Which of the following performers did not see postseason action with the 1944 St. Loo world champs? Blix Donnelly, Johnny Hopp, Ken O'Dea, Coaker Triplett, Al Jurisich, Augie Bergamo. Double.

7 Cards fans can't blame him for the Red Sox sweep in the 2004 Series, as he topped all Mound City regulars with a .357 BA against Boston and belted the Birds' only two homers. Acquired that August to boost the offense, he's a clean single.

8 Stan Musial tagged just one round-tripper in his four fall appearances. It came in Game 4 of the 1944 classic off a 35-year-old Brownie right-hander who was a rookie that year as per current frosh rules. Name Stan's yearling victim for a solo shot of your own.

9 What Card became the first NL rookie to lash two homers in one Series game? Never much of a power threat, he punched just four jacks in 422 at bats during the regular season. However, both of his Fall Classic blasts came against that year's AL Cy Young winner. Single for the Redbird and an extra base for his victim.

10 Knowing the Hall of Famer who was shelled in his two appearances with the Cards in the 1928 Series to the tune of a 19.80 ERA rates a two-bagger.

11 Less than a month shy of his 44th birthday, this warhorse appeared in four Series games with the Cards. He had previously played in just one other Fall Classic, 17 years prior as an 18-game winner for an AL flag bearer. Single, plus a RBI for the year he saw Series action as a Bird.

12 What Cards Hall of Famer hit .167 in the first six games of a Series and, after injuring a finger and dropping a fly ball, rode the wood for what proved to be their World Championship clincher? Double for him, RBI for the year, plus two bonus ribbies for knowing the Bird who supplanted him in the field that day.

13 In six years he played with five different clubs and served two stints with the Cards, and in 1964 he stroked a Series record-tying three pinch hits, including the go-ahead single in the opener. An outfielder who batted right and threw left, this Texan will take you to third.

14 Despite his starting and losing Games 1 and 6 of the 1931 Series, the Cards still defeated the A's. Although he was subsequently a four-time 20-game winner in the NL, none of those prime seasons came in Redbirds livery. Who is he for a two-bagger?

15 After an 0-for-11 start at the plate one fall, this Mound City scrapper rebounded, slamming eight hits in his next 11 at bats to earn Series MVP honors. Bunt single, plus a gift RBI for the year.

AB: 15
Hits: 15
Total Bases: 30
RBI: 11

ANSWER SECTION

GAME 1

INNING 1: RED-HOT ROOKIES

1. Three Finger Brown; 1903.
2. Gene Stechschulte; 2001.
3. Bob Caruthers and Dave Foutz; 1884.
4. Albert Pujols, who slugged .610 in 2001.
5. Stan Musial; 1942.
6. Wally Roettger.
7. Alan Benes; 1996.
8. Matt Morris; 1997.
9. Harvey Haddix; 1953.
10. John Fulgham, in 1979.
11. George Watkins.
12. Stan Yerkes.
13. Jesse Haines.
14. Eddie Morgan, Walt Alston, and the pitcher was Lon Warneke.

INNING 2: WHAT WAS THEIR REAL HANDLE?

1. Otis.
2. Roscoe.
3. Albert.
4. Constantino.
5. Eldon.
6. Wilmer.
7. Vernal.
8. Jose.
9. John.
10. Charles.
11. Glenn.
12. George.
13. Harry.
14. Solomon.

15. David, and his middle name is Jonathan, making his true initials the opposite of those by which he is known.

INNING 3: MASTER MOUNDSMEN

1. Bob Gibson; 1961–1966.
2. Ted Breitenstein; 1893.
3. Bob Forsch; 1977.
4. Bill Doak; 1914 and 1921.
5. Woody Williams; 2003.
6. Matt Morris; 2001–2005.
7. Bill Sherdel.
8. John Denny; 1976.
9. Ted Breitenstein; 1894.
10. Umm, did you bite on Brown, who tied for the club lead in 1903? It was Curt Simmons.
11. Cy Young; 1900.
12. It's tempting to say 1968, but it was 1970 when he went 23–7 (.767) and bagged his second Cy Young.
13. Kid Gleason, in 1892–1893.
14. Bob Tewksbury; 1992.

INNING 4: GOLD GLOVE GOLIATHS

1. Hope you didn't say Keith Hernandez, because it's Bill White, 1960–1965.
2. Ken Boyer; Clete with Atlanta.
3. Taylor Douthit, with 547 in 1928.
4. Jim Edmonds; 2000–2005.
5. Bill Doak.
6. Bob Gibson; nine, all consecutively, 1965–1973.
7. Doc Bushong; 106 games in 1886.
8. Dal Maxvill; 1968.
9. Bill Sarni.
10. Leo Durocher.
11. Mike Shannon.
12. Del Rice; 1952.
13. Keith Hernandez, who retired with 11 Gold Gloves earned as a first baseman.
14. Charlie Comiskey at first base.

INNING 5: RBI RULERS

1. Joe Medwick; 1937; 154.
2. Mark McGwire, who sent home 73 mates in 236 at bats; 2000.

3. Rogers Hornsby; 1922.

4. Ted Simmons.

5. Curt Flood.

6. Dots Miller; Honus Wagner.

7. Mark McGwire, who drove home 147 in 1998 and 1999.

8. Tip O'Neill; 1887.

9. Orlando Cepeda, with 111 in 1967.

10. Enos Slaughter, who broke Jim Bottomley's old club mark in 1953.

11. Brian Jordan; 1996.

12. Rogers Hornsby, Jim Bottomley, Joe Medwick, and Stan Musial.

13. Dal Maxvill.

14. Walker Cooper; 1943; New York Giants.

INNING 6: PEERLESS PILOTS

1. Tony La Russa in 2004, when the Cards won 105 games.

2. Charlie Comiskey, with the 1885–1888 St. Louis club of the American Association.

3. Johnny Keane.

4. Jack Hendricks, in 1918.

5. Red Schoendienst.

6. Chris Von der Ahe.

7. Joe Torre, 1991–1993.

8. Ned Cuthbert.

9. Ken Boyer.

10. Marty Marion; he was the Browns' last pilot before they moved to Baltimore.

11. Rogers Hornsby.

12. Eddie Dyer; 1946.

13. Branch Rickey.

14. Billy Southworth.

INNING 7: HOME RUN KINGS

1. Enos Slaughter, in 1942 and 1946.

2. Jim Bottomley, Joe Medwick, Ripper Collins, and Johnny Mize.

3. Jack Clark; 1987.

4. Tip O'Neill; 1887.

5. Chick Hafey, 1928–1930.

6. Ted Simmons.

7. Ed Konetchy; Rogers Hornsby.

8. Gary Gaetti; 1996.

9. Charlie Comiskey, with 25.

10. Did you bite and say Big Mac? It was Ray Lankford, with 204 to McGwire's 191.

11. Bones Ely.

12. Jim Edmonds, with 89; 2003.

13. Rogers Hornsby; 1922.

14. Todd Zeile; 1991.

15. Mark McGwire, with 29 in 2001.

INNING 8: STELLAR STICKWIELDERS

1. No, not the Rajah—it was Jesse Burkett.

2. Vic Davalillo, in 1970.

3. Don Padgett; 1939.

4. Mark McGwire had 383 total bases and hit .299; 1998.

5. Klondike Douglass; .327 in 1897.

6. Willie McGee, with 216; 1985.

7. Curt Davis; Johnny Mize, in 1939.

8. Mike O'Neill, brother of Steve.

9. Rogers Hornsby; .303.

10. Roger Connor. His 138 career homers remained the record until Babe Ruth broke it.

11. Orlando Cepeda; 1968.

12. Ripper Collins.

13. Scott Rolen; Albert Pujols; 2004.

14. Bobby Wallace; 1899.

15. Red Schoendienst stroked 1,980 hits with the Cards; he led the NL with 200 in 1957 while playing for the Giants and Braves but led neither club in that category.

INNING 9: FALL CLASSICS

1. Who said Lou Brock? It's Orlando Cepeda.

2. Six. There were no off days for travel and the Series lasted six games.

3. Dick Hughes, in 1967.

4. John Tudor.

5. Tommy Thevenow. It was the last home run of his 15-year career that finished in 1938.

6. Tim McCarver; 1964.

7. Curt Welch; 1886.

8. Steve Carlton.

9. Detroit Wolverines; 1887.

10. Lou Brock and Mike Shannon.

11. Wattie Holm.

12. Tony Womack, in 2004.

13. Rabbit Maranville; shortstop.

14. Tuesday. The Series, as per usual, began on a Saturday and the teams traveled to St. Louis after Game 2 on Sunday, making Monday an off day.

GAME 2

INNING 1: STELLAR STICKWIELDERS

1. Don Blasingame.

2. Perry Werden.

3. Felix Jose.

4. Rogers Hornsby, Jim Bottomley, and Chick Hafey; Hornsby and Bottomley were with the Browns and Hafey was in Cincinnati in 1937.

5. Garry Templeton; 1979.

6. Rogers Hornsby and Jim Bottomley were with the Browns and Chick Hafey was on Cincinnati in 1937.

7. Lou Brock, with 121.

8. Harry Walker, in 1947; the Phillies.

9. Bobby Byrne.

10. Ozzie Smith, who collected 144 hits in 1986.

11. Tommy McCarthy.

12. Fernando Vina; 2000–2001.

13. Stan Musial (five times); Red Schoendienst and Joe Cunningham.

14. Ed Konetchy.

15. Yank Robinson; 1888.

INNING 2: TEAM TEASERS

1. 1998; Mark McGwire (70), Ray Lankford (31), Ron Gant (26), and Brian Jordan (25).

2. Pittsburgh, Cincinnati, and the Los Angeles Dodgers.

3. 1968, when the Birds hit .249.

4. Their cross-town rivals, the St. Louis Browns; 1944.

5. 1897; Boston.

6. 1974; Reggie Smith (.309), Bake McBride (.309), and Lou Brock (.306).

7. 1914; Bill Doak.

8. Their .578 winning percentage was the lowest to that point by a NL flag winner.

9. 1976; Hector Cruz.

10. 1942–1944.

11. 1885–1888.

12. Helen Robison Britton, the niece of deceased owner Stanley Frederick Robison.

13. 1946–1949. The Brooklyn Dodgers lost the first NL pennant playoff series ever to the Cards on the final day of the 1946 season and clinched the 1949 flag by a one-game margin over the Birds on the final day of the 1949 season.

14. 63 games back; the 1897 and 1898 teams.

15. 1986.

INNING 3: CY YOUNG SIZZLERS

1. 1899.

2. Flint Rhem, in 1926.

3. John Tudor; 1985.

4. Dizzy Dean, when he won 30 in 1934.

5. Bob Caruthers; 1885.

6. Bob Tewksbury; 1992; Cy Young, in 1900 at 1.01.

7. Surprise! It's Al Hrabosky, who notched nine in 1974.

8. Dizzy Dean and Ted Breitenstein.

9. Sam Jones, in 1958.

10. Bruce Sutter.

11. Pete Alexander; 1927.

12. Dizzy Dean.

13. Lee Smith; 1991–1992.

14. Ernie Broglio; 1960, before he was traded for Lou Brock.

INNING 4: BULLPEN BLAZERS

1. Lee Smith; 1991–1993.

2. Lindy McDaniel, in 1960.

3. Jason Isringhausen; 2004; 47 saves.

4. Ted Wilks; 1946–1947.

5. Joe Hoerner, 1966–1969.

6. Dave Veres; 2000–2002.

7. Bobby Shantz; 1963.

8. Ray King; 2004–2005.

9. Dizzy Dean, with 30.

10. Jeff Lahti.
11. Bill Sherdel.
12. Hal Haid.
13. Bruce Sutter; 1983–1984.
14. Al Brazle.

INNING 5: WHO'D THEY COME UP WITH?

1. Philadelphia Phillies; 1978.
2. Reds; 1929.
3. Nope, not the Phils—the 1939 Cardinals.
4. Boston Red Sox; 1979.
5. Giants; 1919.
6. Houston Astros; 1976.
7. New York Giants (then known as the Gothams); 1883.
8. Cleveland Indians; 1962.
9. Cubs; 1943.
10. Chicago White Sox; 1975.
11. Phils; 1942.
12. New York Mets; 1983.
13. Buffalo Bisons of the NL; 1880.
14. Phils; 1940.
15. New York Yankees; 1986.

INNING 6: FAMOUS FEATS

1. Larry Jaster, who dominated the Dodgers in 1966.
2. Wilbert Robinson, who managed Brooklyn in 1924 after recording 11 RBI in an 1892 game.
3. Red Schoendienst; he batted right; Detroit southpaw Ted Gray, who took the loss.
4. Keith McDonald; 2000.
5. Rogers Hornsby; 1922.
6. Woody Williams; 2003; Rafael Furcal.
7. Johnny Lush.
8. Did you say Mark McGwire? Ouch—it's Jack Clark, who drew 136 walks in 131 games; 1987.
9. Stan Musial (from 1957 to partway through 1970); Gus Suhr and Billy Williams.
10. Rogers Hornsby, in 1922; Jesse Burkett, with 240 in 1896.
11. Dick Schofield; 1953.
12. Stan "the Man" Musial, in 1948.
13. George Crowe, in 1959 and 1960.

14. Joe Medwick, Tip O'Neill, and Rogers Hornsby with two; 1887 for O'Neill, 1937 for Medwick, and 1922 and 1925 for Hornsby.

15. Hi Bell; 1924.

INNING 7: MEMORABLE MONIKERS

1. Dennis Eckersley.
2. Stanley Bordagaray.
3. Enos Slaughter.
4. William Doak.
5. Al Hrabosky.
6. Marty Marion.
7. Walter Arlington Latham.
8. Erv Dusak.
9. Arnold McBride.
10. Harry Lowrey.
11. Emmet Heidrick.
12. Ozzie Smith.
13. George Fisher.
14. Clarence Childs.
15. Miller Huggins.

INNING 8: FORGOTTEN UNFORGETTABLES

1. Silvio Martinez.
2. Tom Alston.
3. Kent Bottenfield; 1999.
4. Lou Klein, whom Chandler banned after he jumped to the Mexican League in 1946; 1951.
5. Austin McHenry.
6. Garrett Stephenson; 2000.
7. Bill Keister; John McGraw; 1900.
8. Estel Crabtree, who grew up in Crabtree, Ohio.
9. Ray Sadecki; 1964.
10. Joe Presko and Tom Poholosky.
11. Roger Freed; 1977.
12. Charlie James.
13. Jack Harper; Cincinnati.
14. Von McDaniel; 1957.

INNING 9: PEERLESS PILOTS

1. Rogers Hornsby.
2. Gabby Street.

3. Stan Hack.

4. John McCloskey; 1906–1908.

5. Jim Bottomley, who took over the Browns during the 1937 season.

6. Tim Hurst; 1898.

7. How many bit on Fohl or Von der Ahe? It was Fielder Jones, who piloted the Browns and the Federal League St. Louis Terriers.

8. Eddie Stanky; 1954.

9. Ray Blades.

10. Miller Huggins and Branch Rickey.

11. Jack Krol.

12. Pat Tebeau; 1899, when the team finished fifth in a 12-team league.

13. Vern Rapp, in 1977.

14. Solly Hemus; 1959.

GAME 3

INNING 1: SHELL-SHOCKED SLINGERS

1. Jason Marquis; 2006.

2. Nelson Briles; 1966.

3. Ted Breitenstein; 1894.

4. Mark Mulder; 2006.

5. Bill Hallahan; 1930.

6. Jerry Reuss, in 1971.

7. Dizzy Dean; 1935 and 1936.

8. Al Jackson; 1966.

9. Red Ehret; Louisville.

10. Pol Perritt and Dan Griner.

11. Kent Mercker; 1998–1999.

12. Harry and Gerry Staley; 1959 White Sox.

13. Brett Tomko; 2003.

14. Murray Dickson; 1948.

15. Red Donahue; 1897.

INNING 2: HOME RUN KINGS

1. Johnny Mize, 1939–1940, and Mark McGwire, 1998–1999.

2. Tom Brunansky; 1988–1989.

3. Ken Boyer and Whitey Kurowski.

4. Ray Lankford.

5. Terry Moore, with 80.

6. Ron Gant, in 1996.

7. Rogers Hornsby.

8. Jack Stivetts.

9. Bill White, with 27 in 1963 and 24 in 1965.

10. Milt Stock.

11. Fernando Tatis, whose club record was tied by Scott Rolen in 2004.

12. Emil Verban.

13. Oscar Walker.

14. Carl Sawatski and Gene Oliver.

15. Dick Allen; 1970.

INNING 3: MASTER MOUNDSMEN

1. Toad Ramsey; 1890.

2. Nelson Briles, in 1968.

3. Gerry Staley.

4. Bruce Sutter, who had 25 saves for the Cards in the 1981 strike year, when they won just 59 games.

5. Jesse Haines; 24 wins; 1927.

6. Kent Mercker.

7. Alpha "Al" Brazle.

8. Ernie Broglio, in 1960.

9. Jack Taylor, who completed all 67 of his starts with the 1904–1906 Cards.

10. Darryl Kile; 2000.

11. Kid Gleason; 1892 and 1893.

12. Curt Simmons; 1963–1964.

13. Ed Murphy.

14. Jumbo McGinnis.

15. Kid Nichols, who posted a 9.17 mark in 1904.

INNING 4: NO-HIT NUGGETS

1. Ray Washburn; 1968; he held the Giants hitless after his team was no-hit the day before by San Francisco's Gaylord Perry. It was the first time in ML history two teams took turns no-hitting each other in consecutive games.

2. Bobo Holloman of the AL Browns, in 1953, and Ted Breitenstein of the AA Browns, the Cards' ancestors, in 1891; Bumpus Jones, with Cincinnati in 1892.

3. George Nicol, nicknamed "Kid" after Kid Nichols.

4. Ted Simmons, in 1971 and 1978.

5. Jesse Haines, who faced the Boston Braves.

6. Jose Jimenez; 1999.

7. Paul Dean in 1934, after his brother Dizzy threw a three-hitter in the first game.

8. Bud Smith; 2001.

9. Bob Forsch, in 1978 and 1983; Ken Forsch.

10. Lon Warneke, "the Arkansas Hummingbird"; the Cubs.

11. Jesse Burkett was shut down by Christy Mathewson in 1901.

12. Tim McCarver.

13. Bob Gibson, in 1971.

14. Don Cardwell.

INNING 5: WHAT WAS THEIR REAL HANDLE?

1. Charles.

2. Gregory.

3. D'Arcy.

4. Howard.

5. William.

6. James.

7. Glenn.

8. Elieser.

9. Harry.

10. Terry.

11. Earl.

12. Thomas.

13. George.

14. Elvin.

15. Pack. Gibby changed his birth name from Pack to Robert, which had been his middle name.

INNING 6: CIRCLING THE GLOBE

1. Joe Quinn.

2. Edgar Renteria.

3. Tip O'Neill.

4. Mike Gonzalez.

5. Miguel Cairo.

6. Charlie Getzien.

7. Bobby Fenwick.

8. Kurt Krieger.

9. Hugh Nicol.

10. David Green.

11. David Brain.

12. Danny Cox.

13. Moe Drabowsky.

14. Sidney Ponson; 2006.

15. Patsy Donovan.

INNING 7: STELLAR STICKWIELDERS

1. Miller Huggins, with .402.

2. Johnny Hopp.

3. If you thought we were trying to sneak Hemus past you, you fell into our trap. Instead we caught you leaning the wrong way on Ray Blades at .395, three points higher than Hemus.

4. Tommy Glaviano.

5. Jack Smith.

6. Not Walker Cooper but Bob O'Farrell, with 213 in 1926, the year he was named the NL MVP.

7. Bones Ely; .463 in 1894.

8. Jack Fournier.

9. Jack Crooks; 1892.

10. Joe Orengo.

11. Emmet Heidrick.

12. Denny Lyons, with a .900 OPS in 1891.

13. Frankie Frisch.

14. No, not Ed Konetchy—Tommy Dowd, in 1898.

15. Edgar Renteria; 2003.

INNING 8: RBI RULERS

1. Joe Torre; 1971.

2. Dizzy Dean; Bob Gibson.

3. George Hendrick; 1980–1984.

4. Ten.

5. Ray Jablonski.

6. Ken Boyer, who hit .293 with 1,001 RBI as a Card.

7. Joe Medwick; 1934–1939.

8. Pedro Guerrero, in 1989.

9. George Watkins.

10. Red Murray.

11. Marty Marion.

12. Charlie Comiskey, with a .300 OBP as a first baseman.

13. George Crowe.

14. Ken Boyer, in 1960.

INNING 9: RED-HOT ROOKIES

1. Rick Ankiel; 2000; Al Kaline.

2. Ed Konetchy.

3. Todd Worrell; 1986; set a new frosh save standard (since broken) with 36.

4. Greg Mathews.

5. Silver King; 1887.

6. Terry Pendleton; 1984.

7. Emil Verban; 1944–1946.

8. Vinegar Bend Mizell.

9. Homer Smoot.

10. Al Brazle.

11. Charlie Peete.

12. Joe Garagiola.

13. Ted Breitenstein.

14. Rip Repulski, Wally Moon, and Bill Virdon; 1953–1955.

GAME 4

INNING 1: JACK OF ALL TRADES

1. Albert Pujols.

2. James "Jimmy" Brown.

3. Mike Shannon.

4. Stan Musial won during seasons in which he played first base and all three outfield slots.

5. Joe Torre played third base in 1971.

6. Johnny Hopp.

7. Todd Zeile.

8. Art Hoelskoetter.

9. Yank Robinson.

10. Ken Oberkfell.

11. Rick Ankiel and Kid Gleason.

12. Mike Tyson.

13. Pepper Martin.

14. Jose Oquendo; 1988.

15. Ken Boyer; third base; and what may come as a tad of a surprise to many—center field!

INNING 2: MEMORABLE MONIKERS

1. Tony Pena.

2. William Shannon.

3. Roy Cromer.

4. Bert Jones.

5. William Perritt.

6. Richard Clapp.

7. Harry Walker.

8. Tom Sullivan.

9. Jim Bottomley.

10. John Miller.

11. George Whitted.

12. Bill Hallahan.

13. Ennis Oakes.

14. Emerson Hawley.

15. Bill McGee.

INNING 3: TUMULTUOUS TRADES

1. Curt Flood.

2. Bugs Raymond and Red Murray.

3. Ray Sadecki went to the Giants for Orlando Cepeda in 1966.

4. Ozzie Smith and Garry Templeton.

5. Joe Medwick and Curt Davis.

6. Pitchers Ernie Broglio and Bobby Shantz and outfielder Doug Clemens.

7. George Hendrick.

8. Ron Northey.

9. Wally Westlake.

10. Burleigh Grimes.

11. Pete Alexander.

12. Lon Warneke.

13. Steve Carlton, Jerry Reuss, Mike Torrez, and Fred Norman; Jose Cruz was the outfielder.

14. Gene Paulette.

15. Willie McGee; Bob Sykes.

INNING 4: TEAM TEASERS

1. 1985; John Tudor and Joaquin Andujar.

2. The 1941 team finished second to the Dodgers with 97 wins; Sam Nahem.

3. Jake Beckley.

4. 1957.

5. 1963; Dick Groat, Bill White, and Curt Flood.

6. 1929.

7. 1987; Bob Forsch, Danny Cox, and Greg Mathews.

8. 1918. Rogers Hornsby finished second.

9. 1969.

10. 1982, when the Cards whacked just 67.

11. 1930.

12. 1967; Dick Hughes.

13. 1980, the year after Lou Brock's retirement; Red Schoendienst.

14. 1931; Bill Hallahan.

15. 1904; Kid Nichols, with 21, and Jack Taylor, with 20.

INNING 5: BRAZEN BASE THIEVES

1. Pepper Martin.

2. Bobby Tolan, who led with 57 steals for the 1970 Reds.

3. Patsy Donovan.

4. Frankie Frisch, in 1927; New York Giants.

5. Garry Templeton; 1977–1978.

6. Tom Herr; 1985.

7. Red Schoendienst; 1945.

8. Jack Smith.

9. Vince Coleman, who stole 107 for the 1986 Cards and batted just .232.

10. Charlie Comiskey.

11. Terry Pendleton; third base.

12. Red Murray.

13. Ivey Wingo.

14. Joe Torre; 1969; Orlando Cepeda.

15. Johnny Mize, in 1939.

INNING 6: MOMENTS TO REMEMBER

1. Fernando Tatis; Chan Ho Park.

2. Specs Toporcer.

3. Sonny Siebert.

4. Red Schoendienst; 1951.

5. Adam Wainwright, in 2006.

6. Mike Ryba, born in DeLancey, Pa.; Bill DeLancey.

7. Reggie Smith; 1976.

8. It came in the final major league game ever played in Robison Field, the last wooden park in the majors and the Cards' home before their move to Sportsman's Park.

9. Mike O'Neill.

10. Nippy Jones was the hitter, and Adrian Zabala, the Mexican League jumper, was the pitcher.

11. Jim "Pud" Galvin.

12. Peanuts Lowrey.

13. Burleigh Grimes, who pitched on the 1930–1931 Cards pennant bearers.

14. Mark Whiten; 1993.

INNING 7: PEERLESS PILOTS

1. Hope you didn't say Eddie Stanky or Solly Hemus. It's Harry Walker; Walker replaced Stanky during the 1955 season, Boyer's rookie year, prior to which Stanky had retired as a player.

2. Jack Hendricks.

3. Bill McKechnie; 1928.

4. Branch Rickey, Rogers Hornsby, Gabby Street, Marty Marion, and the toughie, Jimmy Burke.

5. Kid Nichols; 1904, when he won 21.

6. Gabby Street, in 1931.

7. Mike Jorgensen, in 1995.

8. Fred Hutchinson.

9. Nope, not Frankie Frisch—Patsy Donovan.

10. Shame on you if you said Hornsby. It was the man who replaced him as the Cards skipper: Bob O'Farrell, in 1927.

11. Whitey Herzog.

12. Mike Gonzalez.

13. Roger Bresnahan, 1909–1912.

14. Fred Dunlap, the UA batting king in 1884, when he finished the season at the wheel of the St. Louis Maroons; he also later managed the Maroons after they joined the NL in 1885.

INNING 8: RED-HOT ROOKIES

1. Johnny Beazley; 1942.

2. Ted Wilks; 1944.

3. Vince Coleman; set the rookie stolen base record with 110 in 1985.

4. Tommy Long.

5. Johnny Mize; 1936–1937.

6. Eddie Kazak.

7. Eddie Yuhas.

8. Leon Durham; 1980.

9. Gus Mancuso.

10. Bill McGee.

11. Showboat Fisher; 1930.

12. Ken Burkhart.

13. Arnold Hauser.

14. Lon Warneke.

INNING 9: FALL CLASSICS

1. Lonnie Smith; Royals, in 1985.

2. Sparky Adams; Jake Flowers and Andy High.

3. Anthony Reyes; the Tigers' Justin Verlander in 2006.

4. Clarence Mitchell.

5. Ken Dayley.

6. Joe Medwick, Pepper Martin, and Ripper Collins.

7. Ken Boyer.

8. Johnny Beazley.

9. Jesse Haines; Ernie White.

10. Tom Lawless.

11. Like Johnson, he made only two starts and won his third game in relief.

12. Tony Pena.

13. Frank "Creepy" Crespi, who broke his leg twice during World War II, the second time in a wheelchair race; Jimmy Brown.

14. Jeff Suppan.

15. Jim Bottomley; Chick Hafey.

GAME 5

INNING 1: ALL IN THE FAMILY

1. Jose, Hector, and Tommy Cruz; 1973; Jose Cruz Jr.

2. Andy and Alan Benes; 1996 in Game 4 of the NLCS.

3. Max and Hal Lanier.

4. Chris Duncan, in 2006, when papa Dave served as the Cards pitching coach.

5. Todd and Mel Stottlemyre Sr.; 1996 and 1964, respectively.

6. Ron and Scott Northey.

7. Ducky and Dick Schofield.

8. Bill and Jack Gleason.

9. Olivares; Omar and Ed.

10. Mort and Walker Cooper.

11. Ed and Scott Spiezio; 1967 and 2006, respectively.

12. Joe Delahanty.

13. Bobby Crosby, who took top honors with Oakland in 2004; his father Ed.

14. Red and Marty Marion.

INNING 2: RBI RULERS

1. Milt Stock.
2. Nope, not Stan the Man. It was Jim Bottomley; 1928, when he also became the only batsman ever to collect as many as 30 home runs and 20 triples in the same season.
3. Enos Slaughter; 1952.
4. Stan Musial; 1958.
5. Ray Blades.
6. Rogers Hornsby and Stan Musial; 1922 and 1948.
7. Del Ennis.
8. Albert Pujols drove in 130 at age 21; 2001.
9. Lou Brock, with 814.
10. Enos Slaughter; 1952.
11. Rogers Hornsby, 1916–1922, and Ted Simmons, 1972–1978.
12. Mike Shannon, in 1968.
13. Chick Hafey; 1928–1930.
14. Yep, Curt Flood, with 528.

INNING 3: CY YOUNG SIZZLERS

1. Matt Morris; 2001, when he won 22.
2. Silver King; 1888.
3. Lindy McDaniel, in 1960.
4. Mort Cooper; 1944.
5. Chris Carpenter, who went 21–5 (.808); 2005.
6. Darryl Kile, in 2000.
7. Red Barrett; 1945.
8. Joaquin Andujar; Dominican Republic.
9. Howie Pollet, in 1946.
10. Andy Benes; 1996.
11. Bill Doak.
12. Joe Magrane, in 1989.
13. Harry Brecheen; 1948.
14. Would you believe it's Gibson again, in 1970 at 3.12?

INNING 4: ODD COMBO ACHIEVEMENTS

1. Bob Gibson, who surrendered 5.84 hits per nine frames in 1968 and tossed 108 career wild pitches.
2. Arlie Latham.
3. Lee "Specs" Meadows.
4. Vince Coleman, who was nabbed 25 times in 1985 and later swiped 50 straight in 1988–1989.

5. Jim Bottomley.
6. Lance Painter.
7. Steve Evans.
8. Ted Simmons.
9. Jack Harper; 1901.
10. Bill Gleason.
11. Ozzie Smith.
12. Jimmy Brown.
13. Dizzy Dean.
14. Lou Brock.

INNING 5: MVP MARVELS

1. Frankie Frisch.
2. Ken Reitz, who played in 1,100 games as a Cardinal.
3. Miller Huggins.
4. Dots Miller.
5. Rogers Hornsby; Giants.
6. Dizzy Dean; 1934.
7. Ken Boyer; 1964.
8. Stan Musial; 1943 and 1946.
9. Tom Henke; 1995.
10. Gregg Jefferies.
11. Joe Torre; 1971.
12. Stan Musial, Enos Slaughter, and Howie Pollet; Dixie Walker of the Dodgers.
13. 1974, when he set the former modern record for steals in a season with 118.
14. Gabby Hartnett.

INNING 6: HOME RUN KINGS

1. Charlie "Home Run" Duffee.
2. Ken Boyer; 1960.
3. Andy Van Slyke, who led the Cards in homers in 1986.
4. Whitey Kurowski.
5. Rogers Hornsby; 1925 and 1922.
6. Joe Medwick, in 1935.
7. Sparky Adams.
8. McGwire must have tempted many, but it's Tino Martinez, who hit 21 in 2002.
9. Steve Bilko (.746) and Ray Jablonski (.735).
10. Mark Whiten, in 1993.

11. Rogers Hornsby; 1925.

12. Homer Smoot.

13. Ozzie Smith; 1987.

14. Stan Musial, Rogers Hornsby, Jim Bottomley, Enos Slaughter, and good for you if you identified Lou Brock as the fifth.

15. Hope the "don't walk" steered you off Walker Cooper, because it was Del Rice.

INNING 7: RED-HOT ROOKIES

1. Ray Jablonski.

2. Mike Torrez; 1969.

3. Ron Willis, in 1967.

4. Charlie Gelbert.

5. Gene Green.

6. Mike Donlin.

7. Joe McEwing; 1999.

8. Verne Clemons.

9. Joe Hoerner; 1966.

10. Solly Hemus.

11. Larry Jaster.

12. Ray Washburn; 1962.

13. Oscar Walker.

14. Bake McBride; 1974.

INNING 8: THE NAME'S THE SAME

1. Harry, Bill, and Larry Walker.

2. Dick, Neil, and Ethan Allen.

3. Orlando, Geronimo, and Tony Pena.

4. Dots, Doggie, and Stu Miller.

5. Mike, Tip, and Jack (brother of Mike) O'Neill, in 1902.

6. Mark, Jack, and Will Clark.

7. Sam, Cowboy, and Nippy Jones.

8. Joe, Barney, and Buddy Schultz.

9. Sparky, Buster, and Babe Adams.

10. Bill White.

11. Spike, Wally, and Mike Shannon.

12. Billy, Si, and Alex Johnson.

13. Ron, Chuck, and Carl Taylor.

14. Buster, Jimmy, and Tom Brown.

15. Jimmie, Chief, and Preston Wilson.

INNING 9: MASTER MOUNDSMEN

1. Slim Sallee, who was 106–107 as a Card. Note that Bob Caruthers, Silver King, and Dave Foutz all won 100 when the franchise was still known as the Browns.
2. Max Lanier.
3. Mort Cooper (2.77), Max Lanier (2.84), Harry Brecheen (2.91), and Dizzy Dean (2.99).
4. Bill Doak.
5. Syl Johnson.
6. Steve Carlton; 1971.
7. Bill Sherdel.
8. Jesse Haines; 1920.
9. Silver King, in 1888.
10. Curt Simmons; 1966.
11. Bob Forsch; 1975–1980.
12. Donovan Osborne, who won 13 in 1996.
13. Rick Wise, in 1972 and 1973.
14. John Tudor; 1985.

GAME 6

INNING 1: BRAZEN BASE THIEVES

1. Terry Moore.
2. Joe Medwick; 1938.
3. Jack Smith.
4. Jim Bottomley, with 50.
5. Bob Gibson, with 13.
6. Tony Scott, in 1979.
7. Ray Lankford snagged 44 in 1991 and 42 in 1992.
8. Ozzie Smith, who snared 433.
9. Lonnie Smith.
10. Willie McGee, who was nailed just 97 times.
11. Miller Huggins, with 36 in 1914.
12. Gregg Jefferies; 1993.
13. Surprise! It was Ken Boyer with 85, not Pepper Martin, who bagged nearly half of his 146 career thefts while serving at other positions.
14. Delino DeShields (whose stolen base total includes one as a PH); 1997; Montreal Expos.
15. Rogers Hornsby; 1922.

INNING 2: STELLAR STICKWIELDERS

1. Lou Brock; 1967.
2. Joe Torre, with 352 in 1971.
3. Willie McGee, who hit .353 in 1985 and .256 in 1986.
4. Mark McGwire; 1998, reached base 320 times and hit .299.
5. Jason Marquis; 2004–2005.
6. Cesar Cedeno; 1985.
7. Lou Brock; 1979.
8. Patsy Donovan, with .314.
9. Keith Hernandez; 1979.
10. Curt Flood, who set the righty mark with 178 in 1964.
11. Gregg Jefferies, with .342 in 1993.
12. Julian Javier.
13. Bill White, 1962–1964.
14. Keith Hernandez, who just missed at .299.
15. Pedro Guerrero; 1989.

INNING 3: MEMORABLE MONIKERS

1. Sylvester Donnelly.
2. William Robinson.
3. Leo Durocher.
4. Tom Parrott.
5. James Davis.
6. Joe McEwing.
7. Elton Chamberlain.
8. Bob Duliba.
9. William Dillhoefer.
10. Bob Caruthers.
11. Enrique Calero.
12. Charles McFarland.
13. Lonnie Smith.
14. Frank Snyder.
15. Harry Brecheen.

INNING 4: BULLPEN BLAZERS

1. Steve Kline; 2001.
2. Cris Carpenter.
3. Harry Gumbert.
4. Paul LaPalme, with 57.
5. Mark Littell, in 1978.
6. Slim Sallee; 1919 Reds.

7. Ted Wilks, who led in 1949 and 1951.
8. Bob Bowman.
9. Clyde Shoun; 1939–1940.
10. Jim Brosnan and Larry Jackson.
11. Al Hrabosky; 1975; tied Lindy McDaniel's club standard set in 1959.
12. Todd Worrell; 1986–1988.
13. Billy Muffett, with seven wins and 13 saves.
14. Dennis Eckersley; 1996–1997.
15. Phil Paine.

INNING 5: GOLD GLOVE GOLIATHS
1. Curt Flood; 1966.
2. Jack Smith.
3. Fernando Vina; 2001–2002.
4. Hugh Nicol.
5. Curt Welch.
6. Start blinking—it was Steve Bilko, in 1953 with 124 assists, the club record until 1979.
7. Ozzie Smith; 11.
8. Chuck Diering.
9. Bobby Shantz; 1962.
10. Tom Pagnozzi, who bagged his first in 1991.
11. Mike Matheny; 2003.
12. Joaquin Andujar; 1984.
13. Terry Pendleton, at third; 1987.
14. Steve Kline, from 2001 through 2004, played in 300 games with the Cards without ever making a miscue.

INNING 6: SHELL-SHOCKED SLINGERS
1. Bill Kissinger, 1895–1896.
2. Danny Jackson; 1995.
3. Jesse Haines; 1929.
4. Andy Benes; 2001.
5. Sal Maglie.
6. Lindy McDaniel; 1961.
7. Wee Willie Sudhoff.
8. Bob Purkey; 1965.
9. Jack Stivetts.
10. Jose DeLeon; 1990.
11. Lon Warneke.

12. Ray Sadecki; 1964.
13. Dave LaPoint.
14. Bill Steele.
15. Kip Wells and Anthony Reyes, in 2007.

INNING 7: HEROES AND GOATS

1. Bob Gibson.
2. Game 7 was originally scheduled for October 14, 1946, but was postponed by bad weather to October 15, giving Brecheen an unexpected day of rest and enabling him to win Game 7 in relief.
3. Ozzie Smith.
4. Willie Sherdel, who went 0–2 in 1926 and 1928.
5. Barney Schultz.
6. Murry Dickson.
7. Ozzie Smith and Jack Clark; Tom Niedenfuer.
8. Pepper Martin; Mickey Cochrane, against whom Martin swiped five bases in 1931.
9. Tip O'Neill; .435 in 1887.
10. Gordon Richardson.
11. Ripper Collins; 1934.
12. Jesse Haines.
13. Jim Bottomley.
14. Dal Maxvill; 1968.
15. Steve Balboni.

INNING 8: WHAT WAS THEIR REAL HANDLE?

1. Max.
2. Denton.
3. Arnold.
4. William.
5. We throw one of these in every now and then just to keep the crowd honest—it was Debs.
6. Thomas.
7. George.
8. Eldred.
9. Dorrel.
10. James.
11. Charles.
12. Bodhi.
13. John.

14. Arthur.

15. Dying to know the real first name of anyone who'd prefer to be called Bruno? It was Christian.

INNING 9: FALL CLASSICS

1. Billy Southworth.

2. John Stuper; 1982.

3. 1946; the 25-man player limit was lifted that year to accommodate returning World War II vets.

4. Erv "Four Sack" Dusak.

5. Ron Davis.

6. Marv Owen; Chick Fullis.

7. Bill Hallahan.

8. Darrell Porter, in 1982.

9. Jeff Weaver, in 2006.

10. Scott Rolen, Yadier Molina; 2006

11. Red Munger.

12. Roger Maris.

13. Billy Southworth again, with the 1924 Giants; as manager of the 1948 Boston Braves.

14. Nippy Jones; Milwaukee, in 1957; Joe DiMaggio.

GAME 7

INNING 1: RBI RULERS

1. Bill White, in 1962.

2. Tom Herr; 1985.

3. Todd Zeile in 1993; like Torre, he began as a catcher.

4. Jim Edmonds, who set the team batter whiff mark in 2000.

5. Jocko Milligan; 1889.

6. Jake Beckley; 1906.

7. Joe Medwick; 1934.

8. 1920, when he tied for the lead with George Kelly.

9. Frankie Frisch.

10. Reggie Smith.

11. Todd Zeile, with 103 in 1993.

12. Ray Sanders; 102 in 1944.

13. Ozzie Smith; 1987.

14. Ripper Collins, with 128 in 1934.

INNING 2: MVP MARVELS

1. Keith Hernandez; 1979; Willie Stargell.
2. Lonnie Smith, in 1982.
3. Dizzy Dean; 1934–1936.
4. Dick Groat; 1963.
5. Bob O'Farrell; 1926.
6. Tim McCarver; Orlando Cepeda; 1967.
7. Bob Gibson; 1968.
8. Mort Cooper, Enos Slaughter, Marty Marion, and Walker Cooper.
9. Willie McGee; 1985.
10. The low game total should have steered you to a catcher, in this case Walker Cooper.
11. Whitey Kurowski.
12. None other than Stan, on four different occasions.
13. Albert Pujols; 2005.
14. 1978.

INNING 3: RED-HOT ROOKIES

1. Reggie Cleveland; 1971.
2. Hector Cruz; 1976.
3. Otto Krueger.
4. Ken Oberkfell; 1979.
5. Lee Magee.
6. Willie McGee; 1982.
7. Bill DeLancey; 1934.
8. Dick Hughes, in 1967.
9. Stoney McGlynn.
10. Don Lang.
11. Stu Miller; 1952.
12. Les Bell.
13. Brooks Lawrence; 1954.
14. Pug Bennett; 1906.

INNING 4: WHO'D THEY COME UP WITH?

1. Phillies; 1911.
2. New York Mets; 1995.
3. Cubs; 1915.
4. Indians; 1951.
5. Oakland A's; 1996.
6. Washington Nationals; 1897.

7. Boston Braves; 1952.

8. Oakland A's; 1971.

9. Cincinnati Reds; 1937.

10. Chicago Cubs; 1938.

11. California Angels; 1993.

12. Milwaukee Brewers; 1971.

13. Cincinnati Reds; 1912.

14. Seattle Mariners; 1993.

15. St. Louis Browns; 1932.

INNING 5: STRIKEOUT KINGS

1. Nope, not Carlton. It was Toad Ramsey; fanned 257 in 1891.

2. Jack Stivetts, who led the AA in 1891.

3. Matt Morris; 2001–2005.

4. Bill Hallahan; 1931–1932.

5. Jose DeLeon; 1989, when he whiffed 201.

6. Fred Beebe; 1906.

7. Lynn McGlothen; 1974.

8. Harry Brecheen, in 1948.

9. Bob Forsch, who fanned 1,079.

10. Jesse Haines.

11. Chris Carpenter; 2005.

12. Bill Sherdel, Harry Brecheen, Bill Hallahan, Slim Sallee, Max Lanier, Ted Breitenstein, Vinegar Bend Mizell, and Howie Pollet.

13. Sam Jones, with 225 in 1958.

14. John Tudor, who reached a career high of 169 in 1985.

15. Three Finger Brown; 1903.

INNING 6: STELLAR STICKWIELDERS

1. Frankie Frisch; 1930.

2. Jack Clark, in 1987.

3. Taylor Douthit, 1929–1930.

4. Albert Pujols, in 2003.

5. Johnny Schulte.

6. Jim Edmonds; 2004.

7. Were you caught between Rogers Hornsby and Stan Musial? It's Albert Pujols, from 2003–2005.

8. Tip O'Neill.

9. Joe Torre; 1970–1971.

10. Chick Hafey and Jim Bottomley were the Cards, and Bill Terry of the Giants finished second in the race.

11. Garry Templeton; 1977–1979.

12. Dick Cooley, also known as Duff, though he was seldom called that in his day despite being mistakenly listed that way in most reference books.

13. Edgar Renteria; 2004.

14. George "Doggie" Miller.

15. It's false. Hornsby's 253 total bases as a shortstop in 1917 were nine short of Bobby Wallace's total of 262 in 1899.

INNING 7: HOME RUN KINGS

1. Stan Musial; 1948 and 1949.
2. Ken Boyer; 1961–1964.
3. Buster Adams; 1945
4. Joe Medwick, with 31 homers and 56 doubles; 1937.
5. Edgar Renteria, with 71.
6. Reggie Sanders; 2004–2005.
7. Les Bell, with 11.
8. Ray Lankford, with 228, edges Big Mac by eight.
9. Reggie Smith; 1974; Jack Rothrock, with 11 in 1934.
10. Bill White; 1961–1965.
11. Tip O'Neill.
12. David Green.
13. Lou Brock, who hit 129 homers.
14. Joe Cunningham, with a .856 OPS.

INNING 8: MASTER MOUNDSMEN

1. Jose DeLeon, in 1989.
2. Bill Hutchison.
3. Dizzy Dean, 1935–1936, and Joaquin Andujar, 1984–1985.
4. Mort Cooper, with 105 victories and a .677 winning percentage as a Card.
5. Bob Gibson; 1965–1966.
6. Howie Krist.
7. Howie Pollet, who first topped the NL in ERA in 1943.
8. Stoney McGlynn; 1907.
9. Bugs Raymond; 1908.
10. Joe Magrane, with five wins; 1988.
11. Dizzy Dean, Jesse Haines, and Mort Cooper.
12. Max Lanier, who had jumped to the Mexican League; 1946.
13. Pete Vuckovich; 1982.
14. Bob Gibson (23) and Rick Wise (20); 1972.

INNING 9: FALL CLASSICS

1. Bill Hallahan and Tex Carleton; Bill Walker.
2. Tim McCarver.
3. Marty Marion.
4. Tito Landrum.
5. Red Schoendienst.
6. Coaker Triplett.
7. Larry Walker.
8. Sig Jakucki.
9. Willie McGee; Pete Vuckovich.
10. Pete Alexander.
11. Jim Kaat; 1982 after going 1–2 for the Twins in the 1965 Series.
12. Chick Hafey, the NL bat champ that year; 1931; Ernie Orsatti.
13. Carl Warwick.
14. Paul Derringer.
15. David Eckstein; 2006.

ABOUT THE AUTHORS

David Nemec is among the best-selling baseball writers in the United States. His *Great Baseball Feats, Facts and Firsts* has sold over 700,000 copies in various editions, the most recent of which was coauthored with **Scott Flatow**. Between them, Nemec and Flatow have won ten National Trivia Contests sponsored by the Society for American Baseball Research.